No Such Thing as False Hope:
Surviving Brain Cancer

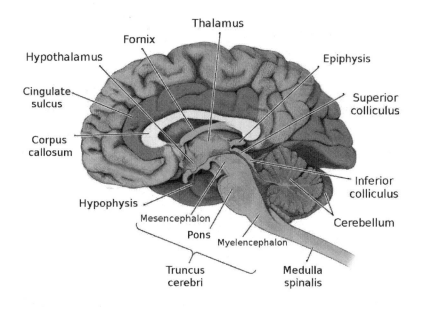

Joy, Marty and Elise Pentz

ISBN- 9781980433774

Dedicated to Dr. Jessica, who makes Elise feel like she is her only patient. When other doctors were giving up, she said Elise's chances were not zero, and because of that Elise is still alive six years later.

Reflections on My Brain Cancer Journey

Forward by Elise Pentz

People give me so much credit for surviving brain cancer. I don't think it's deserved. The whole time I was in the hospital, I was so messed up from the tumor that I wasn't really there.

It was much harder for my parents. I really just followed directions. Although I wanted to kill myself, and tried to, I always wanted to stay alive also. It was a weird push and pull between those two parts of me.

I also didn't like the narcotics given to me because they always made me throw up, which I guess is a blessing in disguise, allowing me to stay clean and mildly serene during it all.

It was kind of nice being in the hospital because I had all my needs taken care of by other people. It was also relaxing to just lay around all day, because I was so fatigued. The only time I remember being scared was when we were at the brain surgeon's office in early 2012 waiting for the diagnosis and when Dr. Y finally told us, I wasn't really sure what it meant. I had to ask my parents, "Does that mean cancer?" When they said yes it wasn't that scary.

I guess I always just assumed I'd get through it. I had survived addiction, so it didn't seem that daunting. I really appreciated the support and love from my parents, my boyfriend (at the time) and my friends. I never felt alone during any of this. My depression kind of helped with that because it was easier to hope for death than to hope for life.

One thing I remember about rehabilitation is that a nurse or transport tech left me by myself in my wheelchair in an empty hallway. I really had to use the bathroom. I had been picturing walking by myself so hard that I thought I could just get up and walk to a bathroom. I was wrong. I got up and my legs fell out from under me.

I just lay on the floor yelling "Help!" for the next five minutes. I started crying and finally someone found me. I felt so pathetic. That was probably the worst experience during rehab because I felt completely powerless over everything. I couldn't get back in my wheelchair. I couldn't control what was going on in my head. I couldn't do much of anything. The only thing I could do was ask for help. Thankfully someone heard me and they were so nice. I kept saying I felt so pathetic and they said "Oh honey, it's okay." I was so relieved that they were kind.

Another time I felt super pathetic was when I didn't make it to the bathroom in time and my Occupational Therapist had to clean me up. I felt horrible for her and embarrassed. I'm so grateful for the Physical Therapists for teaching me how to walk again so I don't have to feel that way ever again as long as I keep walking and doing what I'm supposed to do. I'm even driving now which is really miraculous considering I couldn't move myself from the floor without help. What a blessing this all has been.

When I was out of the hospital and dealing with real life again, it was a weird re-introduction into the world. I felt like a totally new person and I wasn't sure how to handle anything. I resumed my "regular" life of going to my fellowship meetings, working the program and hanging out with my boyfriend whenever he wasn't busy. We've broken up after six years, and I feel okay with that. I think the cancer drastically changed our relationship and we never really discussed it. I'm grateful to be alive today and everything else is just bonus. I also have a newfound faith in a higher power that I sometimes call God. I am content with my life and grateful to have survived two life threatening diseases, addiction and cancer.

Forward by Elise's brother, Daniel

Was I hopelessly optimistic or just delusional?

Or maybe the above is just a false dichotomy, but I never wavered from my conviction that Elise would pull through.

Part of that was based on the data: Individuals with her tumor are typically either very young or very old. Elise was neither; she was a healthy, athletic teenager. Oh and tough. From day one. I vividly remember Elise getting her toddler vaccinations; she shrugged off the injections without so much as a whimper and looked at the medic giving the injections with contempt. Yes, in later years we would tease Elise about crying over misshapen pie pieces, "It's not a triangle!" or getting teary eyed because her playground swing trajectory wasn't perfectly aligned, and she was too young to be able to tell us why she was crying. But she was always strong when it mattered. And never did it matter more than during her ordeal.

Maybe I never wavered because I never sensed her waver. In fact, in relative terms, she held up better than nearly everyone else in the family. Maybe it was her irrepressible sense of humor and ability to make light of her own situation. There were so many "maybes" during Elise's ordeal but the only definite was my faith in her.

Forward by Elise's sister, Emily

I first found out something was wrong when I received a phone message from my Dad, which he struggled to finish because he was breaking down in tears. My experience of Elise's cancer journey has felt strange because of the geographical distance separating me from my family. During the darkest moments of anguish and the daily struggles of rehabilitation which they all experienced first-hand, I was absent. I tried to be involved by contributing to CaringBridge comments and following the updates, but I was no different than the other people following Elise's progress who were not immediate family. That being said, I am amazed and grateful for the strong and supportive network of friends and family that Elise and my parents were able to call upon in their hours of need. Settling down in another country, however exciting and romantic it may seem, certainly has its drawbacks, which I didn't foresee in my naiveté. Being present for your family's ups and downs and experiencing them first-hand is impossible when you live elsewhere; I haven't grown closer through this difficult experience, as the rest of my family did. That being said, I was able to at least contribute to bringing some happy news to my family with the announcement and development of my first pregnancy.

I decided to visit Elise before I was too close to my due date to safely travel overseas. I was also urged by a work colleague who had lost a brother to brain cancer to visit Elise while she was still doing okay. Elise is very intuitive and sensed my purpose; my mom overheard her telling a cancer support worker that I was there to visit her before she died. I hadn't thought of it quite in those terms, but there was some truth in her impression. During my visit home I had the embarrassing accomplishment of beating Elise at putt-putt because her double-vision had returned that day. Little did any of us know that this was the start of a very quick downward turn. It had been lovely being home and sharing my pregnancy with my family—Lilia just started to move and kick during my visit home.

I had phone calls and CaringBridge updates during the most life-threatening time of Elise's cancer journey. I told a few people about what my sister and family were going through—some understood the gravity of the situation because they had known people with brain tumours, all of whom had not survived. I remember crying a lot when I would look at the family photos decorating our window sill, contemplating the time when I might have to tell my future child that the young girl in the photo 'was' my sister. I also remember attending some of the events at the annual village festival where we lived, which included some church services and singing. I had to leave the service after a few minutes because I couldn't stop sobbing and had quickly run out of tissue. I still find I get choked up most times when I sing— I guess I can't help but think of the joy Elise found through singing and the fact that she isn't able to participate in it as she would like to as a result of the cancer.

I know my parents' and brother's experience of Elise's cancer journey was far, far worse than mine—the stress of which was constantly visible on my parents' faces during our Skype calls, even when we were talking about non-cancer topics. I can see now that they have healed a little from the trauma but that they continually battle against fear and uncertainty. I think we are all dumbfounded at Elise's miraculous recovery—she has experienced more in 25 years than some of us may ever experience in a lifetime. I am so proud of her and encouraged by her new vocational rehabilitation assessment and plan, working toward smaller, more achievable goals in order to accomplish her ambitions. We love you!!!

Forward by Elise's Dad, Marty

Elise was born 29 February 1992, and the exquisiteness of love was born out again. Her birth deepened my love for Daniel and Emily, Joy's two children from her first marriage. I feel like Dad to all of them. We had what I would call normal challenges in raising three children with an 8 and 11 year difference between Elise and her sister and brother. Then came addiction and the fateful day of December 10, 2011 - Day 1 of a journey of love, deep anguish, fear and tremendous highs. While my sanity has been challenged my faith in God has continued to grow.

One does not expect to be discussing do not resuscitate orders (DNR) with doctors about your 19-year-old daughter, but that is just one of the gut wrenching decisions Joy and I had to make. December 10, 2011 started like many Saturdays at that time of my life. I met a friend for coffee, went to a park to read for a while then went to meet Elise and Drew for lunch. We found out how quickly life can change. As the story of Elise's cancer unfolded, we found out the critical importance of love from family and friends, (love in the form of prayer, food, chores at home etc.). We also became acutely aware of the need for good health insurance, which we have, and a host of caring healthcare professionals, especially Dr. Jessica and Dr. B. I work at a VA hospital, and the doctors there, both MDs and PhDs, answered all my questions willingly. I realize now I was looking for added kernels of hope.

To conclude this introduction I will tell two stories from this journey. When Elise was the most ill, May of 2012, and I did not think she would live (but had hope) between Joy, Drew and I we would not leave her alone in the Neuro Intensive Care Unit (NICU). As one might guess I was not sleeping well so I took the middle of the night shift. I would hold Elise's hand and sing Psalms to her in the middle of the night. As painful as this time was the singing of Psalms to her was also exquisitely beautiful. In the very early morning, 0500 or so, I would sit at a pond behind the hospital and talk with God while watching the geese.

Memorial-day weekend 2012 Elise had been in a coma for a little over two weeks. At times fear seemed to permeate my being and almost consume me. Fear – while it did not, and still has not completely left, I know God was and is with me. My sisters and brothers came to help and they told me later to say goodbye to Elise. Early Saturday morning, 26 May 2012, I entered Elise's room to spell Drew. Prior to this time Elise's eyes would be open, but not responsive to any activity around her. This amazing morning her eyes followed me across the front of her bed. I asked, "Elise you in there" and she gave me a thumbs up. I said "holy f--k" and went out to get her mother. In May of 2012 Elise could not breathe, talk or walk on her own. While there is still a long road ahead, it is ahead. As you will see in the story to follow, the blessing of having a long journey with Elise and healing was accompanied by much, love, hope, help, pain of all kinds and fear.

Forward by Elise's Mom, Joy

We decided to call this book, "No Such Thing as False Hope" because we discovered through this remarkable journey that there is only hope. "False" hope is what doctors are afraid to give us. I guess they don't want us to be disappointed if our hopes are not fulfilled, especially when they don't expect the patient to survive. The truth is, being warned against being hopeful would not lessen the loss. Living through a time of uncertainty, when death is almost certain, hope is the most precious thing to hold on to. We knew there would be plenty of time to deal with loss and grief if death prevailed. There is no amount of warning that would prevent that devastation. But why dilute the feeling of hope with preemptive grief? I knew my hope was not realistic, and that I was not facing reality. I needed to delude myself to get through each day. I could only achieve the state of hope I needed by achieving the delusions I needed to feed the feelings of hope.

I remember the first time a scan showed that Elise's tumor had stopped growing and was actually shrinking. The radiologist who gave us the good news was quick to add, he didn't know what would happen in the future, in a tone that indicated he didn't think the future looked good. Why not let us be ecstatic with that news without trying to temper our enthusiasm and hope? What good does that do? Why not let us have a moment to savor a rare piece of good news? A pessimistic and worrisome view is constantly lurking inside of us. We don't have to be reminded of it, especially if that reminder is not given for the purpose of changing the course of treatment at that point.

At one point, a chaplain asked what plans we had if Elise did not survive. It is totally appropriate to plan for the contingency of your own death by having life insurance and pre-paid funeral arrangements. It is quite another thing for a person who is supporting you in prayer to save your child's life, to ask you to contemplate her death so you can make contingency plans at the same time.

On the other hand, an example of a friend who supported our hope was a co-worker who has an unshakable belief in God that I wish I had. I could always count on her to calm my fears just by the way she cried, "Believe!"

I still need to cultivate my feelings of hope to assuage the fear of losing my child to brain cancer in the future. I realize the prognosis is statistically not good, but no one is a statistic. The statistics are based on past results, and there are no reliable statistics for the combination of treatments Elise received and is still receiving through complementary remedies. (See the Appendix for the complementary remedies we give Elise, with links to information.) These remedies span time and geography to prevent cancer "seeds" from growing by providing "soil" that is not conducive to their growth. It is my understanding that we all develop cancer cells, but we don't all develop cancer.

Brain cancer is so rare, and recurrence so common, that not many doctors ever treat patients who survive long term. But thanks to the internet, patients and their families are able to find each other all over the world. Survivors are sharing their stories and gaining knowledge and strength from each other. I often read stories and updates of long term survivors to stoke my hope, especially when fear and doubt creep in. This is the story of another survivor to give others hope. Please let us know if we are able to do that for you and your loved ones, whether you need hope for cancer or for any other reason.   Any money that may come to us through the sale of this book will go towards providing for Elise's continued survival.

This book is basically a real time account of our continuing journey through brain cancer as told through our CaringBridge, Facebook and email posts to keep our family and friends informed. Elise's CaringBridge site has had 23,586 visits as of March 4, 2018. We have added recent comments to update and clarify. The recent comments are indented. We did not document the details of Day 1 in real time because we were too busy living it. I have recreated it for you here:

The Beginning of Our Journey
December 10, 2011 - Day 1

Elise and her boyfriend, Drew, met her dad, Marty, at Panera Bread for lunch. We now refer to this as the "Panera Bread Incident." Elise was standing in line getting ready to order. She turned around and vomited on the people behind her in line, and started staggering to the bathroom. Marty asked Drew if she had been drinking, and he said, "No, I've been with her all day." He later told us she was stopped the day before because of how she was driving, and he told the police officer the same thing. Marty called me, and I drove to Panera Bread, and we sat in the car discussing what we should do. I figured she had the flu, and there wasn't much they would do if we took her to the ER, but she seemed really sick. I suggested we go to the hospital where we had a sleep study scheduled for her because she had been sleeping so much during the day. We scheduled it at a small hospital in a nearby town because the sleep doctor there was recommended by a friend. The Emergency Room was not crowded at all. Elise kept vomiting as we were checking her in.

They got us to a room, and a Physician's Assistant (PA) examined her and asked her questions. She told him about her sleepiness. She said she had headaches and vomiting the last two days. He asked if she had had a CAT scan yet. When we told him no, he ordered one. While she was getting the CAT scan, I went to the hospital cafeteria to get a bite to eat. I just knew the CAT scan would be fine; they have to run tests just to rule things out. But as I ate, I had the thought that this may be the last time I would enjoy eating, and our world would be totally different if they found something.

I returned to Elise's room, but she was not back yet. Drew had gone outside to call his parents and let them know what was going on. I sat next to Marty and waited. The PA returned. He squatted down by our chairs to our eye level to tell us there was a mass in Elise's brain. My jaw dropped. I asked how big it was and was it operable, and he said, "Whoa. Let's not get ahead of ourselves until we have more information. We ordered an MRI with and without contrast to get a better look." When the MRI was over, the PA asked if we wanted to see the scan, and he took us to a computer to view it. My eyes about popped out and I said, "It's huge!" It was the size of a golf ball deep in her brain.

When Drew returned and we told him about the mass, he got down on his knees by Elise's bed and cried. The PA told us he ordered the scan because Elise took just a few seconds too long for a 19 year old to answer his questions. Another PA or doctor in a busy hospital may very well have concluded it was the flu, and Elise would have been sent home. Brain tumors are so rare, and up until then Elise's only symptom had been sleepiness. They transferred us by ambulance to St Vincent Hospital because she was in danger of falling into a coma. I remember riding in the ambulance assuming having a brain tumor meant she was going to die. The doctor on call told us it looked like a low grade glioma. They don't use the term "benign" for brain tumors. There is nothing benign about having a mass inside your brain. He told us it would cause too much brain damage to operate. He asked about family history, and we told him about the cancer in Marty's family. When he asked if we had any questions I said, "I can tell by the look on your face, that I won't like the answers." I didn't want to ask any more questions.

Meanwhile, Elise was in the Neuro ICU getting steroids to reduce the pressure in her brain, and she was becoming aggressive and agitated. She was too dehydrated for them to start an IV in her hand, so they had to use her neck. She didn't know what was going on, and we heard her screaming down the hall during the procedure. Later, all through the night, the nurses came into her room frequently to check on her to make sure she did not go into a coma from the pressure in her brain.

This was on a Saturday, and we had to wait until Monday for surgery. Marty, Drew and I took turns keeping watch in Elise's room, while the other two slept on couches in the waiting room. I didn't know what to do with myself waiting and worrying. I decided I would crochet little wall hangings for Else's caretakers with their names on them. Not only was it something to keep me going, but it was also a way to honor the people serving her. I admit, I also hoped it would inspire them to care about Elise even more.

We met Dr. Y, the brain surgeon, that morning. I asked him if I could hug him, and if he prayed for his patients. I was clearly not my usual self. He said yes, and we hugged. He told us the mass effect of Elise's tumor caused her third ventricle to be blocked, and the cerebral spinal fluid could not circulate properly, so he was going to perform a third ventriculostomy to reroute it. He was also going to biopsy the tumor. He too thought the tumor was low grade, and said it was too risky to remove a tumor from the thalamus because of the collateral damage it would cause.

He went through the same routine we would witness countless times. "Touch my finger, then touch your nose. Look straight ahead and tell me how many fingers I'm holding up to the side. Extend your arms in front of you and close your eyes." As Elise's left arm drifted down, Dr. Y explained that was because the tumor was on the right side of the brain. Later that afternoon, we watched Elise being wheeled away to have some holes drilled in her head and her brain cut on.

This is the beginning of our real time messages

Sprinkled with updates and later thoughts shown in italics:

>>> JOY PENTZ: 12/13/2011 6:39 AM >>>

All your messages, prayers and support have meant the world to us. Elise's surgery went well. She now has two more holes in her head--the one they drilled through her skull and a new drainage pathway to drain the spinal fluid through the ventricle that is blocked by the tumor. The tumor cannot be removed without risking serious neurological problems. It will take a week or two for the biopsy results. The surgeon believes it is benign and slow growing. If that is the case she will have radiation to stop its growth. He said radiation does not shrink benign tumors as a rule. The tumor did not seem to affect her functioning too much until it blocked the drainage of the spinal fluid causing pressure. I guess she will have one extra golf ball size marble in her head. One in reserve if she ever loses her marbles. Will keep you posted. Thanks again. Joy

>>> JOY PENTZ: 12/14/2011 10:44 AM >>>

Thanks to all of you for all your support and prayers. I'm really sorry I missed seeing some of you who came to visit yesterday. I guess I came down off my adrenaline high and crashed hard and could not keep my eyes open. Elise is much better, but I guess I expected more. Her left side is still weak, she has a constant headache and her affect is flat. We freaked out when we learned that a neurooncologist was going to speak with us. Elise was on the agenda of the tumor board yesterday morning, and based on the MRIs they thought it was best to make contact now just in case. That's when I started to crash. We need more frequent "fixes" from her surgeon who exudes confidence and hope. I don't deal well with uncertainty. Thanks again. Joy

12/14/11 email from Joy to Pike Community Orchestra   If any of you are praying people, please pray and ask your prayer network to pray for my 19 year old daughter, Elise. She had brain surgery yesterday after being admitted to the neuro ICU at St V Sat. She had been sleeping a lot and having a very painful headache, and began staggering and vomiting Sat. The surgeon said the tumor looks to be slow growing and benign, but is in a place too risky to remove.

We won't know the biopsy results for a week or two. The surgery involved re-routing a blocked ventricle so the spinal fluid could drain and relieve the pressure. We are very grateful we took her in right away because she was in danger of going into a coma. She is much better and still improving, but is still weak on the left side of her body, has a constant but much less painful headache and is emotionally flat. She will have physical therapy and radiation to stop the growth if it is benign. We don't know and hope to not have to know the game plan if it is malignant. I went home yesterday for a bit and was very comforted playing violin for a few minutes. Thank God for Ed and PCO for the opportunity to play with an orchestra even at my level. I quit in Jr. High, but always picked it up to lift my spirit in times of need, but without a group to play with and pieces to learn for performances, I was not inspired to play after each crisis passed. Hope everyone has a wonderful holiday season. Look forward to seeing you soon. Joy Pentz, violinist.

12/15/11 email from Joy
I am sending this to everyone in my contact list because it is easier that way. Sorry if it doesn't make sense to you or if you read the update on Facebook or work email. Thanks so much for all of your support and prayers. We just got Elise home from the hospital after neuro surgery to re-route a ventricle so her spinal fluid can drain. We will not have the results of the biopsy until the end of the month, but the tumor board consensus is that her tumor is low grade, slow growing and not malignant. They don't use the term "benign" for brain tumors. She will need radiation for 6 weeks/5 days a week to stop the tumor from growing. If it is malignant they will add chemotherapy to the treatment plan.

She is actually better than before because she had been deteriorating over the last few months as the fluid increased the pressure in her head once the tumor got big enough to block a drainage route. She was in danger of going into a coma from the pressure. She has had morning nausea and sleepiness for several years, so she could have had this tumor, which is now golf ball size, for many years. She will have physical and occupational therapy to make sure she can balance and walk up and down stairs, and she will not be able to be left alone until then. That may take a week or so. We are very grateful. Thanks again. Joy

Comment from Marty, January 20, 2018: Looking back from today, I can see it took me over two weeks to start writing because of fear.

From: Pentz, Marty, Sent: Wednesday, December 28, 2011 8:10 AM
I know I have sent this information to you all recently, but wanted to thank you for all your prayers and support through all of this. Elise is progressing forward daily and is close to functioning normally. We meet Friday with the neuro- surgeon and will find out the biopsy results at that time. Spirits are up for now, but tend to come and go.

>>> JOY PENTZ: 12/30/2011 4:29 PM >>>.
We just saw the neurosurgeon. He is confident the tumor is low grade, but he will do another biopsy Wednesday because the first one did not go deep enough. This time she will not be having the ventriculostomy at the same time so he can use 3D imaging to go deeper more safely. This will just be an overnight stay, and he will use the same pathway as before which proved to be safe. They need to rule out malignancy so they will know whether they need to do chemo along with the radiation. He said the tumor was not invasive and if low grade it can be radiated to kill it and stop it from growing. We are very relieved because he all but said he was positive it was low grade. Happy New Year everyone. Thanks for all your thoughts and prayers. There are people on all 7 continents including Antarctica praying for Elise.

I contacted NSF (National Science Foundation) who contacted McMurdo station at the South Pole. The Protestant congregation prayed and the Catholic congregation did an intention for Elise for Christmas mass.

Comment 12/17/16 by Joy: After I asked everyone I know to pray, people told me they have friends or family in other countries praying for Elise. I was amazed to realize there were people on every continent, except Antarctica, praying for her. I don't consider myself an especially religious person, but I believe in prayer. I understand the expression, "No one is an atheist in a fox hole." It was easy enough to find out how to contact U.S. scientists and their staff at the South Pole. It's probably not a request the National Science Foundation gets very often. It was a long shot, but what the heck? It couldn't hurt.

After the message got to the South Pole, I got an email from a breast cancer survivor, telling me she and her church on ice are praying. They can only spend a short amount of time "on ice." Then they have to rotate with people working in the U.S. She sent Elise a shirt which has become very special to her. It has a picture of the map of Antarctica with a peace sign superimposed on it. There are people from all over the world working and living together peacefully. Maybe it's too cold to fight.

Comment from Marty January 18, 2018: It can be quite shocking to find out how territorial some doctors can be. Cancer patients need advocates to help search out all viable treatment options. The C word is scary, and it is easy to simply follow the guidance of a confident doctor. As a member of the medical profession, I am appalled at our frequent misplaced over-confidence.

>>> JOY PENTZ: 1/4/2012 7:55 PM >>>
Elise had a deeper biopsy today. The surgeon was able to obtain a diagnostic sample from the center of the tumor. It looks benign, but we will have a more complete report in a week or so. The next step will be radiation to stop its growth. Thanks again for your continuous support and prayers. You got us through this!

12/19/16 Comment by Joy: It took from January 4, 2012 to January 25, 2012, to find out the results of the second biopsy. Those three weeks took forever. The biopsy sample had been sent to Pittsburgh to analyze. It took so long because it was sent to several doctors before they came to a consensus. I was on the internet day and night to read all the information I could find about brain cancer statistics and treatment. I wanted to be prepared if we got bad news. I finally became so despondent from reading about brain cancer, I decided to cheer myself up a bit by reading about benign brain tumors.

I came across a website and forum called, "It's Just Benign." The title expresses the frustration of having serious, life changing problems from brain tumors that people think of as just benign. I came across a doctor in New Jersey who did laser ablation MRI assisted surgery on brain tumors. From there, I found out about the same type of surgery being done at Cleveland Clinic. Armed with this new information gleaned from reading about benign brain tumors, I was ready to face either outcome.

Elise told me her surgeon called and wanted her to come in the next day. I knew then, her tumor was malignant because he would have told her on the phone if it was benign. I also knew because during the last conversation I had with the surgeon's PA, I asked if she thought it was taking so long because they just wanted to make sure it was benign. Her pause before answering let me know that was not the case.

We made plans to take Elise to her favorite restaurant after the appointment, and put on our brave faces. The doctor said, "I'm sorry, but the tumor is an Anaplastic Astrocytoma, grade III." (AAIII) We knew that meant cancer, but not as bad as a grade IV Glioblastoma Multiforme. They had already scheduled an appointment that afternoon with Dr. Jessica, the pediatric neurooncologist we had already met, and a radiation oncologist, Dr. L. They also had surgery already scheduled for a few days later. We were stunned that the surgeon said the only side effect from the surgery would be a little weakness on her left side. This was the same surgeon who told us there would be too much brain damage to remove her tumor when he thought it was benign.

We asked him how many thalamic tumors he had removed, and he said none, but no one has removed many. He appeared to be very excited about the opportunity to do this rare surgery. I asked him about laser ablation surgery, and he said he uses a scalpel rather than a laser. I pressed him further about laser ablation, with the emphasis on ablation, but he just tried to convince me it was the same surgery, just with a different tool. This, along with his excitement about doing the surgery, after having said it was too dangerous, made me very wary of letting him do the surgery.

When we saw Dr. Jessica, and asked her about laser ablation surgery, she said she had not heard of it, but feared Elise's tumor was too big. She told us, "I'll support you in whatever decision you make. Make a decision and don't look back." We also asked her about harvesting and freezing some of Elise's eggs so she could have children if the treatment made her infertile. She said that would delay treatment several weeks, and the look on her face told me survival overruled all other concerns right now. Dr. L, the radiologist, was pleasant enough, but when I asked him about doing proton beam radiation, he said they don't use that on brain tumors. We found out later that was not true. Proton beam radiation may cause less damage than the standard radiation.

Comment by Joy, February 8, 2018: I learned some important things from our experience and the experience of other families I met on this journey, whether in person or online. Medical providers will generally present only the options they offer, and patients should be aware that there may be other options available, some of which may be better for them. This may be because there is so much information, it is difficult to keep up with it. In some cases it may be because they want your business. In some cases it may be both. Whatever the reason, it is important to do your own research so that you become knowledgeable about your choices. It is difficult to read the brain tumor forums because you will see many tragic outcomes, but I learned some of the best information from them, including the minimally invasive surgery which saved Elise from some major deficits. In fact, both of the doctors I spoke with who are doing the type of surgery Elise had, were surprised that a neurosurgeon was going to do a craniotomy to remove her tumor. One said, "No doctor would do a craniotomy on this tumor."

Comment by Marty, January 18, 2018: I remember Joy being, at first, reluctant to accept Daniel's offer to come home and probably interrupt his PhD work. I told her we need him and Elise needs him. She agreed. Another example of our loving fellowship is our friend, William, who picked him up at the airport. Daniel's love, humor, intelligence and faith that Elise would recover were of immeasurable help.

11:49am Jan 31, 2011 email from Joy   We are at Cleveland Clinic now. We met with a pediatric neuro oncologist, Dr. T. Elise is having a fancy MRI right now. Dr B will study it this afternoon. If he thinks he can help her with AutoLitt minimally invasive surgery, he will meet with us Wed morning. Will let you know as soon as we find out. There is another doctor who uses similar noninvasive surgery in NJ who we will consult as well. Otherwise we are coming to the conclusion surgery with craniotomy is too risky to her brain functions. Elise is doing OK, but very sleepy. Daniel is with us, which is wonderful. He is supportive, takes notes and asks good questions. He adores his sister. Emily adores her sister as well, and will be making Elise an aunt in July. Elise is so excited about this, as are we. Thanks for everyone's continued support and prayers and suggestions. We are researching all your suggestions.

1/31/12 email from Joy

Dr. B is enthusiastic about Elise's imaging from this morning. Her tumor has not grown and the main nerves don't run through it. The tumor pushed them aside making surgery less risky. The AutoLitt device he developed is minimally invasive so even safer. Keep praying. Your prayers have lifted us.

> *Comment by Joy Pentz, January 1, 2018: AutoLitt surgery is now called Neuro-Blate.*

Marty Pentz, 3:16pm Feb 3

There are times when I am barely holding it together. Thanks for all your love and support. Tears come unbidden. This is my little girl.

2/8/12 email from Joy

Just met with nurse who said surgery would last 7 to 10 hours from the time they take her away to finish, but the actual incision won't start until about 9:00, 2 hours after they take her back. There are a lot of high tech items to do right beforehand.

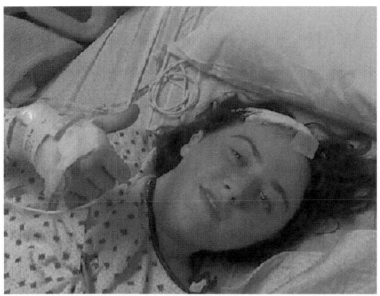

IN RECOVERY ROOM AFTER 10 HOURS OF SURGERY AT CLEVELAND CLINIC

Marty Pentz: February 11, 2012   Elise was able to say, "Hi Dad," a few minutes ago and is eating. As they are supposed to, the ventricles are shrinking so the swelling is going down. She is able to eat. When asked how she was doing she stated "I am irritable," but not much pain.

Joy Pentz, February 11, 2012 ·   Elise is sleeping now with a normal heart rate. It was 150-170 on a consistent basis due to agitation from the steroids she is taking to reduce her swelling. The swelling is causing the blockage of one of her ventricles so they used a cranial access kit to drill a hole to drain the excess spinal fluid which was causing hydrocephalus. They gave her Zyprexa and then Haldol to calm her down and lower her heart rate. She will be here at least a week from today due to these problems.

She is still in ICU. I will be telecommuting next week. Elise has retained her cognitive function except for when the meds impair her. Her left side is getting stronger. Her double vision no longer seems to be constant. I have no doubt she will recover well from this surgery. It is just taking longer than expected due to her reaction to the steroids. She is able to understand and speak Spanish very well. She calms down listening to a recording Emily and Matthew made when they did a benefit concert in Oxford, England to raise money after the earthquake in Haiti. She has even sung a little bit.

I am treasuring this time with Elise; it is nurturing for both of us. I am sleeping very well in a recliner next to her bed each night. I enjoy feeding her too. She cannot use her left hand well enough to feed herself, and her right hand is being restrained to keep it away from the area where the drainage tube is. She ate very well today. She doesn't always remember which hospital she is at; this is her third. She knows she has a birthday coming up, but sometimes she thinks she is 11 or 12. Please keep her in your prayers.

February 12, 2012 · email from Joy

Everything looks so much brighter today. Elise and I had a good night sleep. Her agitation is under control. Her language skills are great considering all the meds. She may need to rememorize her math tables. She was singing a bit spontaneously. She used her left hand to try to scratch her nose, and it is no longer balled up into a fist. She had it scrunched up so tight her thumb was bright red. She is taking smaller doses of steroids and Zyprexa more often to keep her at a steady level to diminish swelling while staying calm.

11:36pm Feb 12 email from Joy

Slowly improving. Elise is still very restless with her meds, but not agitated like she was. She tried to watch TV today, but kept changing channels, not really able to concentrate. She was awake all day until halfway through dinner when she fell asleep mid-bite with the food still in her mouth. All her vital signs and everything are normal. We should know more when we speak to the Dr about the MRI she had today. Thank so much everyone for your thoughts and prayers.

8:22am Feb 15 email from Joy

Dr B said Elise's MRI looked perfect; the surgery worked as planned. The kill line is right up to the edge of the tumor, and the nerve bundles are unharmed. Her double vision is no longer constant. Her cranial pressure is normal. Steady improvement. Thanks for all your support and prayers.

February 16, 2012 email from Joy. Dr B just came by. He is hoping to get the tube out of Elise's head soon and move her out of ICU. He ordered a CAT scan to see the ventricle size. If it looks smaller, and she does ok without steroids, he will remove the tube. He will keep her on Topamax until her 3rd ventriculostomy starts functioning again draining her spinal fluid well. I stopped asking when she might get released because he just says, "One day at a time." He said she was assessed for acute rehab which means in-patient. She will probably go to Hook rehab in Indy.

February 16, 2012 · email from Joy   Elise was confused, sleepy and spacey yesterday. Her left ventricle is enlarged which means her spinal fluid is not draining well. Her dose of Topamax was increased to slow the production of spinal fluid. Right now she is being prepared for an EEG to make sure it is not seizure activity causing her confusion. She told her brother she had alcohol for breakfast and that last weekend was St Patrick's Day weekend. Scary.

February 16, 2012 · email from Joy   Elise has surgery at 10:30am tomorrow to install a shunt to drain her 1st and 2nd ventricle. She will be taken off the Topamax after that. She started having bad headaches again and is not doing well with cognition and balance. The shunt is expected to resolve these issues, and rehab will begin in Indy soon after. I have not been told yet if she is having seizure activity. Thanks for all your prayers and support.

2/18/12 email from Joy   Hi everyone. Elise did well in surgery yesterday. She is answering her status questions correctly most of the time now. She should be transferred out of ICU soon, and then to a rehab hospital in Indy. When she first wakes up she is a bit confused or still in a dream state. Last night I was asking her the names of family members. She said her father's name is Osama. I asked how many years her dad has been sober, and she knew it was 30. I said, so that means he hasn't done what in 30 years? She said, "Attacked." Right after that she knew Marty's name, and that his addiction was liquor, not attacking. Further questioning revealed she knew Osama's full name, and that Obama successfully got him. Even some of the newscasters used to get those names confused! I am not worried about her cognitive functions too much because of the location of the tumor, so it is fascinating to question her. She said she was 6 today, and when I asked her birthday, she held up her fingers for 2/29/92.

> *Comment by Joy. January 20, 2018. I remember during one of Elise's status checks, the nurse asked her where she was. She knew she was in the hospital, and she knew she was at the Cleveland Clinic, but she insisted she was in Wisconsin. She kept saying Wisconsin in an exaggerated Wisconsin accent. I thought maybe she was just being silly, but she got genuinely upset when the nurse tried to convince her that she was in Ohio.*

February 19, 2012 email from Joy· Elise is doing pretty well. She is resting peacefully at the moment. She has a bit of a fever, but Tylenol is helping. She is using her left hand to scratch her nose. (Not that scratching her nose is that important, but her left hand is no longer in a fist.) She can scoot herself up in her bed, so her left side is strong. She is still on Topamax (aka dopamax), so not everything she says makes sense, but she consistently knows where she is, the year and her birthday. She remembers her teachers from elementary school and her soccer team mates. I spent hours getting the EEG electrode glue, blood and tangles out of her hair. I can't believe she let me do it. I enjoyed it so much because she never let me comb her hair when she was little. My sister Carol is in a cab on her way here.

February 20, 2012 · email from Joy   Elise walked with help and she put socks on by herself. She is feisty and witty again. She can carry on a cohesive conversation. These things we don't even think about are complicated functions requiring lots of coordination and brain power. . .

Feb 22 email from Joy. Another update: Elise is getting better by the moment. Tylenol resolved her minor headache this morning. She is able to walk with less assistance. She easily tied her shoes. Her personality is back. When she is tired she is intermittently confused about recent events, but can relate past events accurately. On to the next chapter in her saga.

February 22, 2012 · email from Joy

We are on our way to Hook Rehab from Cleveland Clinic. Elise has lots of different shaved spaces on her head, but her hair is so thick there is only one place that shows so we covered it with flowers from her room. I will make her barrettes with silk flowers to color coordinate with her clothes. You are probably more interested in her medical progress than her fashion update...

DRIVING FROM CLEVELAND CLINIC TO HOOK REHAB IN INDY

February 24, 2012 by Joy Pentz: I like to make positive entries, and there are some positives. However, Elise is feeling depressed, and she has had nausea and vomiting since she was given Percocet for her headache the first day at the rehab. She had been getting that at Cleveland Clinic, but she was also getting Pepcid. We are hoping that is the cause and not a malfunction of her shunt. She does not have headaches every day, and they are mild enough that Tylenol usually works.

Elise said she doesn't want to be institutionalized, referring to the rehab hospital she is at. She also said she feels like she is retarded because the people around her seem that way. She said all she wants to do is sleep, and that she is afraid she will never want to work or go back to college, or if she did want to, she would not be able to. We explained to her that the main reason she is there is because it is not safe for her to walk and use stairs by herself, and because she will get better faster if her therapy is all day rather than short outpatient appointments.

We told her that the location of the tumor mostly affects the muscles on her left side and her ability with mathematical type functions. She was very happy to have some human and canine visitors last night. They really cheered her up. Every Thurs evening volunteers bring dogs to visit the patients. They also have 3 dogs on the unit for therapy. We speculate that Elise has become more aware of the seriousness of her cancer and brain function deficits now that the surgery and shunt have relieved the pressure in the brain, allowing her to think more clearly and be less sleepy and drowsy. She is making such quick progress, we are confident any damage to her brain will not interfere much with her life, unless she wants to be a mathematician.

> *Comment by Marty, January 18, 2018: There was talk during one of her stays at Hook of Elise going to a long-term rehab facility (nursing home) after leaving Hook. I think that would have killed her motivation to get better. I would have quit work to care for her and rehab at home rather than do that.*

By Elise Pentz: February 25, 2012 hey! It's Elise now. Thanks for all of the guestbook entries! Ya'll are so sweet!

Sunday by Elise Pentz, February 26, 2012

Hello all. Today was pretty low key. Just hung out with my parents and Drew. I kept all my food down! Last night my sponsor brought a meeting to me, and it was great :) lots of fun and very helpful spiritually. Me and my mom just watched the videos aunt carol made at the Cleveland Clinic and that was fun.

> *Comment by Joy, February 8, 2018: Elise had become an addict at the age of 15. She always loved being part of her recovery fellowship, but she had not stayed clean and sober without relapses until a year before her brain cancer diagnosis. Next week she will celebrate 7 years of continuous sobriety and clean time, thank God. We are grateful she was not using when she became sick because her brain tumor symptoms of vomiting, staggering and sleeping all day would have been attributed to using. She believes she would have slipped into a coma and died if she had not become clean and sober so that she could realize there had to be another reason for her symptoms.*

February 28, 2012 by Joy Pentz: Elise looked very tired when we visited so I am writing this update. Since Elise is progressing so well, I called the clinic in Houston[1] to see if we could get our March 6 appointment back. I had cancelled it when she was not doing too well at Cleveland Clinic. Our patient coordinator forgot to cancel it before going on vacation, so we were able to get it back. The nearby hotel sales manager forgot to cancel our reservations so that will work out as well. There is a rodeo, so hotels were hard to come by. Elise only has double vision now when she reads. She is moving more easily and can climb stairs, though not safely enough by herself. Tomorrow Elise turns 20. This is her 5th birthday since she was born on leap day.

March 5, 2012 by Joy Pentz.   We are in Houston in a consultation room waiting to meet with doctors. Elise stopped seeing double except when reading a few days ago. Yesterday she starting reading without patching one eye, so her double vision is gone. The bad news is she has more frequent headaches and she is extremely depressed.

March 6, 2012 by Joy Pentz. Elise's depression improved after meeting with the doctors and getting a better understanding of the treatment plan. Today she had a PET scan and an MRI. Now we just have to wait for the FDA to approve Elise for Compassionate Use of Antineoplastons. That usually takes a few days. Then a vascular surgeon will install a port and she will start the treatment. She can go home as soon as Daniel and I learn how to administer the infusions and do the calculations for the pump. Emily is coming home to visit the end of March, and Elise will get to feel her future niece or nephew moving around.

> *Comment by Joy, February 8, 2018: We decided to try Burzynski Clinic is Houston after learning about the dismal survival statistics for the standard of care treatment of chemo and radiation. We were also very concerned about brain damage from radiation, which continues even after the treatment is over because of late effects. Dr. Burzynski's Antineoplaston treatment does not work for everyone, but for those it does work for, there are fewer and less severe side effects, and longer term survival. The treatment had already been through Phase I of FDA approval, which is to explore safety. It had also already been approved in Phase II clinical trials,*

[1] For info re clinical trials: https://www.learnaboutclinicaltrials.org/

which studies effectiveness. The treatment Elise got was in a Phase III clinical trial which compares effectiveness with the standard of care. We knew going in that Elise would be getting the actual treatment.

I spoke with and emailed patients and parents of patients who were long term survivors after this treatment, so we decided to go ahead with it. We had to apply with the FDA for Compassionate Use because patients in clinical trials have to have already failed on the standard of care. In other words, either the standard of care did not work at all or if it worked for a time, the cancer recurred. Compassionate Use allows patients to receive treatment outside of a clinical trial before full FDA approval in cases where the risks to the patient are deemed no greater than the risk of not using the experimental drug. Elise's prognosis with the standard of care was a life expectancy of one to three years.

March 8, 2012 by Joy Pentz: We met with the radiologist yesterday. Elise's tumor has shrunk to 3.1 x 3.5 cm from 4.4 x 4.4 since the AutoLitt procedure! The radiologist said in his opinion looking at the MRI and PET scan together, the tumor is inactive (dead). However, most of the time, her type of tumor "seeds" cancer cells into the surrounding tissue, and these would not be visible with imaging unless they grow. There is still swelling, which was expected. Elise is still struggling with depression and wanting to sleep most of the time. We are working on that from here with the healthcare providers at home. She loves getting your messages, and I hope she will send her own message today.

March 8, 2012 by Elise Pentz: We found out today that the FDA approved me for the clinical trial! Yay! That means we're only in town here until they place my catheter in my central line and teach my mom and brother how to manage my infusions and what not.

March 9, 2012 by Elise Pentz: Currently in the waiting room for installation of my central line with catheter. Took some Atavan and hoping that knocks me out enough to not feel much of their poking. It shouldn't hurt too much according to Chrissy. And she's in nursing school. Still waiting... Should be ready soon. I want pasta. I always do.

March 10, 2012 by Joy Pentz: Elise started on the Antineoplaston infusions yesterday. She has been sleeping even more than before, but that is not unusual. Also she was pretty woozy from the Atavan she took prior to the installation of her central venous catheter yesterday. She is not having any other symptoms, and her depression is improving. She will have 6 infusions per day which will gradually increase in dosage until she is at her maintenance dose on day 16. She doesn't seem to mind having tubing hanging down and having to carry around a bag with the pump and bags of medicine. I told her she will always have an instant conversation starter. She said, "So do you want to know what all this is?"

March 14, 2012 by Joy Pentz: Thanks again for all your encouraging notes. It looks like we can be discharged Friday. We have a 1527 doctor in Indy (FDA form#1527), who will do monthly exams, order blood tests and MRIs. We had to have that before we could leave. Daniel and I have been getting training from a nurse on how to administer the infusions, calculate the volumes, program the pump, change dressing, draw blood, and prepare the bags of medicine and change bags.

Daniel is amazing, and it seems to be transforming his life in a good way. His constant witticisms are so refreshing and lighten the mood. Many patients go to school or work while infusing, wearing the pump and bags in a camel pack on their back. The pump is set up to infuse every four hours around the clock. Between infusions they can be detached as long as a trained person is available to do it in a sterile manner.

Elise's doctors tested her thyroid function to see if that could explain the fatigue and depression. Surprisingly she has hyperthyroidism, too active a thyroid. We are waiting for the results of some further testing to see if it is damage from the tumor or a hormone imbalance, which is easier to treat. In rare cases hyperthyroidism can cause depression, but that too could be damage from the tumor.

Elise's depression has responded somewhat to additional meds, and hopefully it will keep getting better as the levels build up. The infusions are lowering her potassium, so she is on a supplement for that. Hopefully more potassium will help her fatigue. Every morning I ask her to rate from 0 to 10 her headache, nausea, depression and fatigue. Then Daniel asks her to rate how annoying my survey is. If she has a headache or nausea, it is only a 1 or 2, and is helped for the rest of the day by one Tylenol and/or one Zofran.

Her fatigue is usually greater than 5. Her depression has gone from 10 to 5 or below most days.

I am so grateful Elise's mobility and intelligence are pretty much intact. She has trouble with spatial relationships, and sometimes turns the wrong direction, so I told her welcome to my world. I have always been directionally challenged. This is probably more info than you wanted to know, but I guess I'm a bit detail oriented. My family has learned to preface their statements with, "What I am about to tell you is all I know," in an attempt to keep me from asking more questions. Please keep sending the positive thoughts and prayers Elise's way.

March 14, 2012 by Elise Pentz. Hello all! We just went to Whataburger. It was alright. A little too much mustard but whatever. Never been before and my bro wanted to go because it reminded him of Tulsa. We're back at the hotel now. My mom is showering right now and then it's my turn! I have to shower between infusions so it seems like I have limited shower time so I get excited.

March 22, 2012 by Joy Pentz. Hi everyone. Sorry it has been almost a week without an update. It has been a very stressful week mostly because Elise keeps saying she wants to stop treatment because it is inconvenient. She doesn't like the infusion tubing hanging down on her, having to carry the bags of meds and the pump around all day, and being connected all the time. She has had 4 brain surgeries since Dec 10, and she is tired of all of this. Thank God she is not having any side effects from the treatment. She is out with her friends tonight. All her symptoms from the tumor are gone except she fatigues easily and is often sleepy. The radiologist says there is no visible evidence of cancer after the AutoLitt procedure in Cleveland.

This treatment is for any of the cancer cells that may have spread into the tissue surrounding the tumor, which is almost always the case with Anaplastic Astrocytomas. We put Elise's infusion paraphernalia in a backpack instead of a shoulder bag so the tubing won't hang down and the weight will be better distributed. She didn't realize she could be disconnected between doses every four hours for about 2 hours, so that cheered her up a bit. She gets 6 doses in a 24 hour period. We program the pump to start and stop the doses on time. Daniel is her weekday caregiver, and I am her night and weekend caregiver. We will be imparting our knowledge from our training in Houston to Drew and Marty also.

It takes about an hour to prepare the IV bags each day because we have to get every last air bubble out since the bags will not be hanging upside down. We have to draw blood every other day, and take it to the lab. We will take her for MRIs and physicals every month. We speak with our monitor nurse in Houston every day. We have to keep track of the inventory of bags and supplies to order them each month, change her dressing and tubing etc. And Elise thinks it's inconvenient for her! :)

As I told Elise, it is an honor for me to spend this time with her caring for her. It has transformed Daniel as well, and Drew has been the best boyfriend anyone could ask for. We are so grateful that Daniel came back from California to help us. We don't know what we would do without him. He is telecommuting and driving to the University of Illinois to meet with his PhD advisor and research group once a week. He is in computer engineering, and learned to program the pump in a jiff. They were quite impressed in Houston. The pump has two channels for two different meds, so you have to tell it a lot of info. We are so excited to see Emily next week. She is coming from England to spend time with Elise while she can still fly and not have to travel with an infant. We can't wait to feel the baby kick. Please keep your prayers and messages coming. We so appreciate them!

April 1, 2012 by Joy Pentz: Sorry folks. It has been a while. Elise is doing much better. Her energy is up a little, and her depression is stable. We are getting much better at preparing her IV bags in a timely manner, and troubleshooting the pump. Emily is home, and she has been able to coax Elise outside to walk and get fresh air and sunshine. We just finished enjoying a healthy salmon dinner on the back porch with Aunt Kaye. Thanks for all your thoughts, prayers and messages.

April 8, 2012 by Joy Pentz. Thanks for all your encouraging comments, thoughts and prayers. Elise spent some wonderful time with Emily and "the bump". Elise is looking forward to being an aunt, and going to England to spend time with her niece or nephew. We now know if it's a boy his initials will be EMN, and if it's a girl her initials will be LJN. My best guess is Eric Matthew and Lisa Janelle.

We are still going up in volume on Elise's infusions, and her blood tests are still good. It may take a while for her bladder to expand enough to accommodate all the fluid so she doesn't have to worry about being close to a toilet all the time. We are approaching her maintenance dose. She started having double vision again intermittently, mostly outside. Sunglasses help---great idea Emily. Elise and Emily played Putt Putt, and Emily easily beat Elise once Elise began seeing extra balls and holes. (I'm sure Emily would have suggested the sunglasses before she won if she thought of it because that's the kind of person she is.)

Elise has a MRI tomorrow, and hopefully the double vision will be explained by swelling/edema. Most people require steroids during this treatment because of the buildup of pressure in the brain. We are hoping to avoid that because Elise had unpleasant side effects from it. Elise is talking about quitting treatment again, but hopefully she will be encouraged by the MRI (or any reason whatsoever) to continue. Elise is enjoying reading. She just finished Hunger Games, and she is in a book club to read classics. She read The Last of the Mohicans, and started on a Tale of Two Cities. Are there any classics that are funny?

We encourage Elise to watch funny shows because of the medical benefits of laughing and to boost her spirits. I plan to get her the book by Norman Cousins who used laughter to help survive his illness. Elise's fatigue is still a problem, usually a 7 or 8, and she has trouble staying awake. Her depression is generally a 5 or 6. I quit asking her to rate headaches and nausea because they are gone!

> *Comment by Marty, January 20, 2018: Having Emily home at that time was a blessing for all of us.*

April 12, 2012 by Joy Pentz: Thanks for all your wonderful words of encouragement. We really need them. We got the radiologist's report on the MRI, but we have sent the CD of the MRI to the surgeon who did the laser ablation because we really need his expertise to interpret it. He knows what the laser ablation does to the brain and what it looks like as the tumor debulks afterwards. The local radiologist report says, "The appearance of the post contrast images has changed so much that comparison of measurements probably will not be helpful." It also says, "On the prior exam, there appeared to be a single enhancing mass. On today's exam, there appear to be multiple smaller masses surrounding the one central mass. These are not distinguishable on the pre contrast images." That's the scary part, but then it says no new lesions are seen in the brain. Daniel thinks what looks like the multiple smaller masses may be the tumor breaking up and debulking. I like talking to Daniel because he is calm and says I am jumping to conclusions. Stay tuned and please pray hard!

April 17, 2012 by Joy Pentz: It has been a scary roller coaster ride lately. Thanks for all your encouraging words, support and prayers. Elise will have a PET scan tomorrow to see if what looks like smaller masses around the central mass on the MRI is hypermetabolic (indicating cancer). The Cleveland surgeon who knows how to read post AutoLitt MRIs is out until Thursday. The Houston doctor said they didn't know what to make of it...it's weird, so that is the reason for the PET scan. He said the smaller masses are within the borders of the original tumor; that was a relief that it is not spreading outward. Just in case there is new growth, I looked into Proton Beam Therapy. A friend told me about it months ago, and I had asked the local radiation oncologist about it. He said they don't use that for brain tumors. Either he is not keeping up in his field whatsoever or he lied. Either way, we won't be going back to him.

There are only a handful of facilities using Proton Beam Therapy in the country, and one is at IU in Bloomington. It is a form of radiation, but it is more precise in sparing normal cells around the tumor, which is really important in the brain. I spoke with a doctor there, and he was a classmate of Elise's Cleveland surgeon. He said Elise would be a candidate if she does have new growth. He was the nicest doctor. He started out expressing sympathy for Elise, and ended up giving me his direct number as well as his cell number.

Two people asked me to find out if Elise would want to come to their church, one for a healing service by a priest from the Dominican Republic, and the other for healing prayer and touch at St. Luke's Methodist Church. To my surprise, she said yes. She wants to have weekly appointments at St. Luke's. On our way to St. Monica's Catholic Church, Elise said she guessed she would know she was healed if her double vision got better. When we left, it was better, and in a few hours it was gone. Since then it has been intermittent, but it had been constant for several days before that. The mother of the person who invited us, who we had never met before, told me she has been praying for Elise every day at 3:00. That made me cry. I can't tell you how much all of your prayers and support are helping us through this. Thank you.

By Joy Pentz, April 19, 2012 Yippee!!! The PET scan was negative, and negative is good!!! Thanks for all your wonderful messages. We read them over and over for encouragement.

April 26, 2012 by Joy Pentz.   The roller coaster ride is back. We have slightly different takes from various doctors about the MRI and PET scan. Daniel told me I need to parse the words people say with greater granularity. He is right. I hang on every word, pause, inflection and tone of voice trying to figure out what they really mean, and what they are not telling me. I have to find some balance between hope and delusion so that I am not at the edge of tears all the time. Marty was saying he doesn't understand why people sometimes say they don't want to have false hope. He believes there is no such thing. Hope helps. If your hopes don't get realized, you can deal with it then.

Since we found out about Elise's tumor in December, I don't think the shock and denial have been pierced until lately. Now my fear washes over me in waves intermittently throughout the day. Elise has 1-1/4 to 1-1/2 vision just about all the time. It has never been double vision as in seeing 2 of everything. Her fatigue and depression are usually 5 or 6, sometimes 4. Her left hand is curling and she walks towards the left. Her short term memory has not been good the last few days, but that could be due to increasing her Abilify to help her depression. All of her symptoms are consistent with intracranial pressure which can be caused by tumor, swelling from AutoLitt or the high doses of antineoplastons. She is on a low dose of steroids to try to reduce the intracranial pressure.

Marty and I are trying to live in the present, and enjoy spending time with Elise without projecting into the future. I love taking care of her, going on walks with her, talking and singing. She went back to choir last night, which she had lost interest in. It is a bit difficult for her to read the music and words quickly enough for new songs, but when she sings her depression is sometimes lowered by 2 points. Elise told me I'm a good person. I asked if she thought I was a bad person before. She said no, I was just annoying. Then she hastened to clarify that I am still annoying, but a good person. She appreciated my spending $80 to take her to see David Sedaris, a favorite humor author. If you have extra time during the day to walk with Elise, make her laugh, sing with her or just visit that would be great. Thank you for keeping us in your thoughts and prayers.

May 2, 2012 by Joy Pentz: This is really hard you guys! Elise was having symptoms of intracranial pressure as her doses of Antineoplastons (ANP) increased, so we tried low doses of Decadron (steroids). We ended up taking her off both due to side effects. The most upsetting is her confusion. She has only been off the meds for 2 days, so we didn't expect her to return to baseline this quickly. She had a period of time with single vision yesterday, and her bladder symptoms are improving. She said she wants to go to choir again. After she is back to baseline, and we see the results of her next MRI scheduled for May 7, we will try a desensitizing very slow dose of ANP. If that doesn't work we have other options we will try. Please keep praying and sending positive thoughts and messages. It is very comforting knowing there are people all over the world praying for Elise.

May 5, 2012 by Joy Pentz

Elise is about to be admitted to St Vincent's Hospital. We took her to the ER because her symptoms worsened. They did a MRI, and the tumor has grown.

May 6, 2012, by Joy Pentz: Great news!!!!! Spoke with one of the Houston doctors today who said at first we would have to find another option due to tumor growth. Then I read the MRI report to the doctor, and it said the tumor is breaking up. It is larger due to proteinaceous material within a cystic portion and hemorrhage and necrosis (cell death) within the tumor. This is also how the surgeon in Cleveland said the debulking process would occur over months. My understanding is that as the tumor debulks, it will be absorbed by the body, and the cystic portion which is fluid filled should shrink. Elise was released from the hospital as soon as she was able to give a urine sample to rule out infection.

Marty Pentz: May 8, 2012 Elise continues to decline daily. This is so hard and I cry a lot. We are going to start a different round of chemo on Thursday. Nothing we do seems to be helping. This tumor just keeps growing. She has no short-term memory, is forgetting how to eat and has little to no bladder control. She has double and blurred vision. I believe that God is with her through all of this, but I hurt so much. Joy also hurting so, as is Elise's boyfriend Drew. Joy is so loving as she cares for Elise. I have never felt so powerless and my heart aches. We sing with her, mostly Sound of Music and other musicals she loves so, and the Beatles.

May 10, 2012 by Joy Pentz. I have not wanted to update the journal because I want to stay hopeful. When the doctors actually saw the MRI, they said we need to find another option. Everyone is really surprised at how much the tumor grew in a month. Regardless of what kind of cells are in it, it still has a mass effect on the structures of her brain. Elise is getting worse each day it seems. She is having problems with fatigue, memory, walking, seeing and bladder control. Thankfully she does not have headaches or nausea. She will be starting chemo and radiation on Tuesday. I have an appointment with an alternative doctor who has some ideas on ways to protect her from the toxic treatment she is about to receive.

I have decided to stay hopeful no matter what because the alternative is unthinkable, and I can't function well in that dark place of despair. It is such an honor and privilege to be able to care for her. She is so loving and it is wonderful to have this time with her if I can maintain a hopeful state of mind. We pray and meditate and sing together. We are using nutrition, herbs, supplements and other remedies known to have helped some people with cancer. We are continuing to avail ourselves of the healing ministries of churches, which have been so helpful for our spirits. I am very glad my sister, Carol, is coming Sat, and Marty's siblings are coming on Memorial Day weekend.

I am so grateful that my boss is allowing me to telecommute. Work is good for me. The money and health insurance also come in handy of course. Thank you President Obama. I was able to get a handicap placard from the BMV. It didn't occur to me before. I just knew that all the close parking spots around the hospital were handicap spots, and I wished there were some regular ones close by because it is so hard for Elise to walk. Then I had an "I could have had a V8" moment and realized she qualifies. In my defense, I think it was more denial than stupidity. A friend, whose sister has cancer, invited me to go with her to a Wellness Community support group. I know it will be helpful to both of us. We so appreciate your words of encouragement and your prayers.

> *Comment by Joy, January 20, 2018. When Elise and I walked into the Bureau of Motor Vehicles to get her handicap placard, everyone was staring because Elise was walking like a robot, and needed me to hold her up. Her face was expressionless, and her eyes were glazed over. The room was overflowing with people who were waiting to be served. This was before you could renew your license online. When we approached to take a number, a person at the*

counter took pity on Elise, and took care of her placard then and there.

On the way home, Elise was talking to a friend on the phone and told her that we had gone to the dentist, and we were on the way to the beauty shop, neither of which were true. I also noticed that her hearing was failing.

Earlier that day, we had gone to the hospital for an MRI, and the radiologist's office for a special CT scan to enable them to make a wire mask for Elise's head to keep it still during radiation. They were unable to do it because she was could not stay still in the scanner due to another one of her symptoms, which was uncontrollable restlessness. We had to go back to repeat the procedure under anesthesia.

By the end of that day, I was exhausted and sore from the exertion of helping Elise to balance as she walked, and catching her when she fell against me. The other upsetting thing was speaking to a hospital chaplain about Elise's wishes if life and death decisions needed to be made. By this point, Elise could not think clearly enough to have that conversation.

May 13, 2012 by Joy Pentz: Elise is in St. Vincent Neuro ICU. They are asking us questions about DNR and vents. We are crying.

May 13, 2012 by Joy Pentz: Elise is resting easily now. EEG said no seizures, but it's not always accurate. The goal is to get her to radiation Tues and continue chemo. Hopefully the tumor will shrink. Glad to know she can have radiation on a vent if she goes on one. We want to give her every chance at life, but not to prolong it with no quality of life. Members of Elise's choir came in to sing to her. It was amazingly comforting.

May 14, 2012 by Joy Pentz: Elise is now on a ventilator. She is getting steroids to reduce brain swelling. The risk is brain herniation, which would be the end of the road. If she can make it to the morning, we will start radiation and continue chemo. There is a small chance she can get better, but it is not 0, we were told by Dr. Jessica. Please pray for a miracle.

May 15, 2012by Joy Pentz

No change. Elise had radiation today. Her vital signs are good. She is still sedated so we really miss her.

May 16, 2012 by Joy Pentz.   Today was tough. Doc said Elise's heart rate is trending down while her blood pressure is trending up, which could mean pending herniation. After she left the rates normalized, but not after a good cry. We have a DNR (do not resuscitate order) because if her brain herniates it will stop her heart, but getting her heart to beat again would do no good and would be painful and she would die anyway. No parent should ever have to face this. The only way I can get through this is to hope and believe the radiation and chemo will shrink the tumor and restore her brain function. Thank you for your messages, prayers and visits. I don't know what we would do without all of your loving support. .

From: Pentz, Marty   May 16, 2017   Elise continues to hold her own. At this point no progress is a good sign as progress forward may be slow and the reverse fast. She has had no change since the vent went in.

May 17, 2012 by Joy Pentz: No change. All your kind notes, visits, food & flowers have been just wonderful. Keep praying for a miracle.

From: Pentz, Marty Sent: Friday, May 18, 2012 4:32 AM   Friday morning and watching Elise sleep. Joy, Drew and I take turns being present with her. I often sing to her when I am alone with her. Have been singing the Lord's Prayer and my favorite Psalms of praise. Also have been singing, "You are My Sunshine" (one of my mother's favorites that she sang to us as kids.) She looks so content. I love her so.

May 19, 2012 by Joy Pentz: No major changes. Elise's heart rate dropped, but her blood pressure is steady so there is no evidence of pending herniation. Her pupils are not always reactive to light, but she was more reactive to outside stimulus in general throughout the day. For some reason I got through the day without sobbing. I went to bed (hospital waiting room couch) listening to "The Story" podcast about escaping from East Germany, and just woke up to a cancer patient's interview about green burial. I would like that for myself, and if we must face that for Elise, I will discuss it with Marty. That was really hard to write. I do much better believing Elise will be OK.

I joined a cancer support group, and when I discussed my hope as being delusional, the people who have been dealing with this longer told me they look back and realize every day of hope is a gift. For all of you wonderful people who ask what they can do to help, it is to not say anything to pierce my fragile bubble of hope, and to believe and pray for healing. We cannot entertain what ifs. We must live in what is right now, and right now there is still hope. We will face things as they come.

May 20, 2012 by Joy Pentz: Elise's heart rate is higher, which is good. She opened her eyes and Drew and I could see her whole iris. We usually see mostly white. She seemed to be looking at me. Each day that goes by is more painful, but we know going forward will be slow, and going backward would be fast. Keep praying for a miracle.

From: Pentz, Marty: Sent Sunday, May 20, 2012 2:27 AM 2:20 Sunday morning. I just finished singing Lord's Prayer and one Psalm to Elise. No changes and that is good. Will be starting on some hymns shortly. For whatever reason I am at peace right now. Did some crying prior to falling asleep last night. Keep praying

May 21, 2012 by Joy Pentz: No changes.

May 22, 2012 by Joy Pentz.   We are cautiously happy to report that Elise's CT scan today showed no changes. The tumor had been getting bigger every day, so this is a good thing. Also, since her heart rate is low, they thought the scan might show her brain had herniated. It looks like the low heart rate just means she is very relaxed. Thanks for all your kind messages.

Marty Pentz, Sent: Tuesday, May 22, 2012 3:23 AM. Quiet right now. Elise was recently coughing through the vent and all bells and whistles go off. It sure makes this papa nervous. All the nurses and doctors have been telling me this is normal on a vent. Still makes me scared. CT scan later this morning to see what a week has brought us. I continue to hold to the belief that her tumor is shrinking and that between God, Elise, all our love and the meds she will walk out of here eventually. At this point cannot bear the thought of being in this world without her. If that day ever comes will deal with it then. Right now she is here, I am loving her, singing to her and finding some peace among all the machines. Keep praying

From: Pentz, Marty: Sent Tuesday, May 22, 2012 9:00 PM I will get to sleep more tonight and Joy gets up in the middle of the night when Drew is done. CT scan showed no changes as expected, this is a good thing. Will continue to proceed as we have been. She will be getting a trach on Friday as she can only safely have a vent tube for a couple of weeks. She will still be on the ventilator, but through the trach and will still be moderately to highly sedated. She will also have a G tube for feeding and her chemo. All these steps are needed at this time and are easily reversible as the tumor shrinks. It was growing daily and for the past week and a half has been stopped. Now between God, medicine, Elise fighting to live, love from her nurses and all her many friends and our still growing love for all our children this tumor is shrinking. Medicine sees her chances as not so great, but not zero. As a dad right now I am not dealing in statistics, but in that this path has healed others and will heal Elise and I know she is with God.

> *Comment by Marty, January 20, 2018: I remember waiting on these scan results as being excruciating.*

May 24, 2012 by Joy Pentz: No changes with Elise. Regrettably, I asked one of the doctors (not Elise's regular doctor) a question which led to him spewing facts and figures and saying the clinical trial could have made her worse and predicting doom and gloom in a very insensitive manner. I want to be able to believe she will get better. Marty says he just chooses to believe it, and no matter what, she is with God. He said he just does not allow his mind to go the other way because it brings despair. I was able to do that yesterday.

> *Comment by Marty, January 20, 2018: With the prognosis being very poor using standard brain cancer treatment, we chose to try the route of a promising clinical trial. That decision was the best we thought at the time. I am not sure how I would live with myself if delaying the standard treatment would have killed my baby girl. I am blessed that it did not kill her.*

From: Pentz, Marty: Sent Thursday, May 24, 2012 4:52 AM   Slept from 8pm to 3am. Feel good physically. 0445 right now. Elise is peaceful looking and doing well. When this all started the late night time was the hardest for me. Now late at night is the most peaceful of all the day for me. Spoke with Emily yesterday and her pregnancy is proceeding well. Cannot wait for our first grandbaby in England. Hope is alive all over the place for me right now. I have always loved the early morning hours and love them even more now. I appreciate everybody's thoughts, prayers and visits. Marty

From: Pentz, Marty: Sent Friday, May 25, 2012 8:59 AM Elise is remaining stable which is progress at this point. She has been stable since the placement of the vent. As I have stated in the past, progress forward will be slow so we are in a good place. She will have radiation at 10 as usual and then go to OR for trach and peg, these both will make things easier for her ongoing recovery. Looking forward to seeing her whole beautiful face again. She is calm, I am mostly calm and Joy is sleeping. God continues healing our young lady Elise. Anybody coming by that has a Methodist hymnal would be helpful. Joy knows more of the hymns from that hymnal so between the Methodist and Episcopal hymnals we will have it all covered.

> *Comment by Marty, January 20, 2018: Thanks to Dave C. for bringing the hymnal later the same day.*

From: Pentz, Marty: Sent Saturday, May 26, 2012 8:44 AM   After our forced shift change exodus I came back into Elise's room and she had her eyes open, for the first time since prior to admission she followed me when I talked. When I asked her to give me a thumbs up she moved her thumb. She followed the commands of the nurses and wiggled her toes. I ran and got Joy and when Joy asked her to shrug her shoulders she did. She is on the mend. God is good and is healing our little girl. Keep the prayers coming. Marty

May 26, 2012 by Joy Pentz. Thanks be to God! Elise gave us a thumbs up, wiggled her toes, and shrugged her shoulders on command and answered questions yes and no by nodding. She is off the sedation, but still on painkillers, so a bit drowsy. She had a tracheostomy yesterday so she no longer has the breathing tube down her mouth and throat. She won't be able to speak until they remove it when she can breathe better, but she just mouthed "some" when Marty asked if she was hot. I am so grateful and happy!!!

From: Pentz, Marty: Sent Saturday, May 26, 2012 9:22 AM

An aside of humor. Sherry, a friend of Elise's was in the other day and I told her that I have been praying for the shrinkage of the tumor and she said I was the first man she ever heard pray for shrinkage.

May 27, 2012 by Joy Pentz. Another wondrous day. Elise was still responsive, and she was able to breathe for 3 hours without the vent. They put her back on to rest, and will gradually wean her. Marty's siblings, Judy, Pat, Tommy and Ryne are here, as well as my sister Doreen. We are having a wonderful time despite the circumstances. Thanks for all your help, prayers and visits. Thank you choir members for your beautiful singing today. We heard later that one of the doctors here wished you could sing for one of his patients.

May 29, 2012 by Joy Pentz: Elise is the same. We are in a different room because they are fixing the toilet. Then we will move back. She had to be sedated for radiation today, so she is still sleepy. This is really hard. I need to stay grateful for her being responsive instead of disappointed that she is at a plateau right now. Keep praying for a miracle! Thanks!

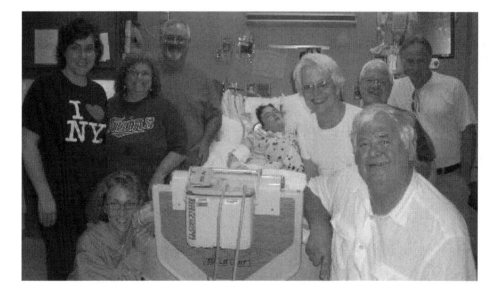

FAMILY MEMBERS CAME FROM MINNESOTA, NEW HAMPSHIRE AND OKLAHOMA TO INDIANAPOLIS TO SAY GOOD-BYE, BUT ELISE "WOKE UP!" PICTURED ON THE LEFT ARE MOM, AUNT DOREEN, AUNT KAYE AND UNCLE TOMMY. PICTURED ON THE RIGHT ARE UNCLE PAT, AUNT JUDY, DAD AND UNCLE RYNE. NOT PICTURED HERE, FAMILY MEMBERS WHO ALSO TRAVELED FAR TO SEE ELISE: AUNT CAROL AND COUSIN AARON FROM NEW JERSEY; DANIEL FROM CALIFORNIA AND EMILY FROM ENGLAND CAME TO SEE THEIR SISTER.

May 30, 2012 by Joy Pentz. We are back in the old room. Elise is still responsive when she is awake, but she is only awake for a few minutes at a time. She is on antibiotics for a urinary tract infection. She is being sedated for radiation each weekday, and remains on Fentanyl for pain, steroids for swelling and Keppra to prevent seizures, so she is pretty drugged up. She spent an hour off the vent today. An occupational therapist worked on her joints, and I repeated the exercises later. We are supposed to do them twice a day. Dr. Jessica was back today. She is so sweet and sensitive to our need to remain hopeful. She was very pleased with Elise's progress. In the category of "give her an inch and she'll want a mile," I was not satisfied with Elise responding to English only. Sat, Sun and Mon I asked her to do things in Spanish, and she did not respond. Yesterday she started to respond to Spanish. What that means to me is higher brain function. She was in Spanish Immersion beginning in Kindergarten, so she has a good command of the language. I just sang to Elise, and I am going to take her peaceful expression as she slept as evidence that she likes my singing. Earlier today I asked her if she wanted me to leave her alone, and she shook her head yes.

June 1, 2012 by Joy Pentz. You can't imagine how much reading your messages helps us. I just changed places with Marty so he is awake with Elise and I am laying on "our" couch in the waiting room to sleep. Elise is so tired, but seemed more alert when she did open her eyes.

June 1, 2012 by Joy Pentz. I just read the updated guestbook. I need to remember to start each day reading it for hope, love and encouragement. Your words are so powerful. Elise was just taken down for her 13th radiation treatment. She is still very tired, but when she opens her eyes they don't roll around in her head ready to quickly close. I do think she closes them purposefully when she gets tired of answering questions. I started asking her if she wants me to leave her alone after a brief interaction, and she always says yes.

Last night I asked her if she knew who I was and she mouthed, "My mom". Although she has been mouthing words for a few days, there was something about the way she answered that really touched me and sustained me through the night.

For those who have been here in the last few days and have noticed that Elise didn't smell as fresh as a daisy, take heart! (Especially Drew) The collar around her neck that holds the trach was saturated with fluids from the wound, getting more foul smelling every day. It has now been changed, and so far there does not appear to be an infection at the wound site or the stuff she coughs up. Watching and hearing her being suctioned out and coughing is quite disturbing. The RTs and nurses said you get used to it. It is getting easier, but I cannot imagine getting used to it. When the nurses repositioned Elise today they said there was some resistance on her right side, which is great because she has not been able to move that side except for barely wiggling her toes on command.

I have been looking at new clinical trials for brain tumors just to have some alternatives for after the chemo and radiation to keep destroying the tumor and prevent recurrence. All the clinical trials are for Glioblastoma Multiforme (GBM), which is the worst kind. Elise's is one step below. I sent emails to two of them to see if they would consider applying for a Compassionate Use exemption from the FDA for her. I got immediate and compassionate replies. One trial uses electrical fields placed on the head to prevent cancer cells from dividing. They told me by email that it is now available commercially and sent a list of doctors trained to use it. I'm not sure if they would use it on her because the FDA approved it for GBM patients over the age of 22. I don't know about "off label" use for devices. The patient has to have a completely shaven scalp, and wear what looks like a bathing cap with embedded disks with cords hanging down attached to a device in a backpack. Walking around like that, you would never need to think of a conversation starter, and I would buy her all the cool hats her heart desired.

The other is a vaccine. They use tissue from the patient's tumor and blood to develop a personalized vaccine which trains the immune system to attack the cancer cells. The woman I spoke with told me it is very difficult to get a Compassionate Care exemption, but they are beginning a new trial in England that Elise could be a part of because the protocol is more flexible there. She would have to be well enough to travel and she would have to have a new biopsy to get fresh tissue. Of course, I am getting way ahead of myself as usual, but I like having additional arrows in my quiver, especially since brain tumors are notorious for recurring.

From: Pentz, Marty: Sent Friday, June 01, 2012 0239 hours Elise has been responsive since Saturday, knows who we are, and has known most of her visitors. I get rather contemplative in these early mornings with Elise. Just now reading about sin being a lack of gratitude for God's gifts. This tumor is not a gift from God, but there have been a lot of gifts surrounding it. Joy and I have given to others throughout the years, now we are receiving much love in the form of visits, hugs, practical gifts like food and my siblings cleaning our house and my brother Ryne cutting our grass. Two weeks ago some church members cut our grass and the day we came to the hospital, almost three weeks ago, some friends from work helped with the yard. In my early to mid-20's I remember being so alone in the world, now I am able to receive and experience God's love all around me and in me. Thanks for all that have helped me continue to become the man I want to be.

From: Pentz, Marty: Sent Saturday, June 02, 2012 9:07 AM 0853. I got to sleep a full night last night. Today marks the end of the third week living here at St. Vincent Hosp, Indianapolis. Was watching two geese and their 4 new offspring this morning and it was beautiful to watch them guard their young, much as Joy and I are doing living at this hospital. Walking back to the hospital I realized this is my life today and that is ok. A quote from one of my favorite books states, "Perhaps one of the greatest rewards of meditation and prayer is the sense of belonging that comes to us." I feel connected to all the people that are praying for Elise and us. More connected to those close to us like family and fellowship friends, but connected to all of you. It is like I can sometimes see or feel a filament or thread that goes out from my heart to all of yours. Elise is better daily, one day at a time.

June 3, 2012 by Joy Pentz.   The nurse just showed me Elise's urine is yellow! Yes! She has had blood in her urine, so it went from red to orange to yellow today. I hope this isn't TMI, but these little things mean a lot. Here's a big thing. Elise has been off the vent since this morning, and we are working on 24 hours. If she can get the trach out she will be able to talk and eat. Another big thing. Last night Elise started moving her left leg and arm. She can squeeze your fingers with her left hand, and can lift her left toes in an attempt to wiggle them. I bet she is so tired of performing all the tricks the doctors and nurses ask of her: Stick out your tongue, shrug your shoulders, raise your eyebrows, squeeze my fingers, wiggle your toes, don't let me push your foot down, don't let me lift your foot.

Elise sat in a chair for about an hour today while the choir members were singing for her. We had a great time. They sang all our favorites, and then some songs from musicals. While we were singing I washed and braided Elise's hair. Elise seemed kind of grumpy today. She is no longer on a Fentanyl drip, so she was probably having withdrawal symptoms. Now she is getting pain meds if she needs it. I started to do her physical therapy on her left hand, and she jerked her arm away from me, seemingly annoyed. I might have been a bit miffed if it was her right arm, but it was great to see the strength in her left arm.

Elise was given a dry erase board made for patients to communicate pain level and all sorts of other things hospital patients might want to say. On one side there is a pain scale and pictures of a body front and back, so you can point to or mark the body part. There are two lists so you can say if the body part is numb, tender, burning, itching, and whether the pain is constant, intermittent, dull, sharp etc. On the other side it has "I am ____(tired, thirsty, hot, lonely, angry etc. I want_____(to be suctioned, to sit up, prayer, lights off, etc.) I want to see_____(doctor, nurse, respiratory therapist, family, etc.) I want to clean_____(face, hair, teeth, etc.) There is a picture of a keyboard with letters and numbers, and a thank you and I love you boxes. There is a blank space where you can write a message. One of her friends (or was it Marty?) said she should just write, "Leave me the f___ alone!" That's probably what she wanted to say to me when she jerked her arm away.

It's hard to believe it has only been a week since Elise started to be responsive again. Each day brings more improvement. It is so hard to be satisfied with the present, and not wonder how she will be down the road. None of us know how we will be in the future. I have to work at being grateful for each moment I have with Elise the way she is right now.

From: Marty Pentz, Date: Sun, 3 Jun 2012 13:52:19 Elise is moving her left side again. Plan is to be off vent for 12 hours or so today and get her into a chair. I see God in all of this. The nurses are very loving and caring and so love Elise. Week ago Saturday when she was aware for the first time in two weeks, one of the nurses jumped up and down and said "hugs all around." Like many in health care this is more than a job for them. I am reminded of another of my favorite quotes from one of my fellowships writings. "True ambition is not what we thought it was. True ambition is the deep desire to live usefully and walk humbly under the grace of God." I see this demonstrated daily in the nurses and other staff and all of our friends that are helping us so wonderfully. Thanks to God and all.

From: Pentz, Marty: Sent Tuesday, June 05, 2012 3:41 AM Elise is sleeping peacefully. Yesterday was difficult as she appears to be withdrawing from three weeks of IV fentanyl. When she has withdrawal symptoms she has difficulty not being on the vent so I had them put her back on the vent until the withdrawal is better addressed. They did this right away. She has been off the vent again since about 1700 last night. It was hard to watch her struggle with withdrawal I know can be better managed, which it now is and will be even better managed once I talk with the ICU Dr. later this morning. Just asked Elise if I could sing to her so sang three Christmas carols and "Morning has Broken." Love singing here to her and God. Have been thinking of my conversations with the nurses, Drs. and other staff and they have become part of my prayer, conversation with God. I talk to God as a supremely loving parent.

Elise is aware even in her sleep. She used to pull on the feeding tube in her nose and now even while sleeping she will scratch around it. Moving forward day by day. 0336 hours. Elise was scheduled to be 12-15 hours off of the vent, but went 18 hours. She is so much better and she said she has hope to be better. Was thinking yesterday about conversations you would not expect to have about your 20 year old daughter, things like the color of her urine, has she had a bowel movement and the most difficult of all DNR or not. She wanted quiet so no singing tonight. Our friends are sharing life with us. I had a great gluten free meal last night brought to us by a friend of Joy's and mine; I have celiac disease. A number of Elise's friends read to her last night and that was great. The active spirituality of our friends has been tremendous. One of my friends of many years ago, Gil Baker, told me that if it is not practical it cannot be spiritual. I take that to mean to be spiritual, an activity has to help oneself or somebody else or what is the point? We have gotten into a rhythm to our life as it is now, one day at a time and sometimes moment to moment. Many blessings tonight, and will be visiting the geese in about 3.5 hours.

June 5, 2012 by Joy Pentz: I was feeling depressed, so I went for a walk in the sunshine and read your messages. My mood improved immediately. Thanks so much for your care and encouragement. Elise is having withdrawal symptoms from Fentanyl, so she is on a more gradual tapering off. She is off the respirator almost all the time, so she no longer needs a constant drip. I finally figured out what she means when she holds up 3 fingers. It represents a "W" meaning whatever. She says it when I tell her I'm sorry she is suffering. I will be so glad when she is totally off the trach and can talk and eat again. Pasta will be a big incentive for her to live. I know that sounds funny, but it is true in her case. Thanks again for your loving words of encouragement.

From: Pentz, Marty: Sent Wednesday, June 06, 2012 3:45 AM 0340 hours. Quiet night. Elise is now in her 33rd consecutive hour of not being on the vent. That is such a wonderful thing. Looks like she will be on the oncology floor by the end of this week. No singing yet tonight, she wants to be left to sleep. God is in this place as everywhere. More later.

June 6, 2012 by Joy Pentz: Two great developments. Elise has been off the respirator for 48 hours, so she should get out of ICU soon and go to a regular room on the oncology floor. Elise wrote, "I want to eat." I will be glad to go to oncology because I think visitors there will be more careful about germs since the patients are immuno-compromised. Elise's visitors have been good about not coming if they are sick, but other patient's visitors have not. Since it is a neuro/trauma ICU, many are coming to say goodbye to their loved ones, so it is understandable. In a regular room there will be a recliner or cot for me to sleep in the room. I'm happy Elise could write, but I feel bad about how it came about. I told her she was getting better, and soon she will get the trach out and be able to talk and eat. Then I made the mistake of telling her about Joey's guestbook message about flying over with the best pasta an Italian can make. Elise has had his pasta, and loves it, so she was angry at me passing on the message since she can't eat right now. I should have known better. Soon after she looked angry and I asked her if she was. She nodded yes, and only at me. I asked her why, and that's when she wrote "I want to eat." Being angry with me is actually progress because she is her sweetest the sicker she is. As always, your messages lifted my spirits. Thanks!

From: Pentz, Marty: Sent Thursday, June 07, 2012 4:04 AM 0351 hours. Quiet again. Went to bed early and actually got 8 hours. Flat affect and no apparent emotional response to what was going on with Elise. She is able to write a little now and stated that she wanted to eat. She also wrote that she was scared. While these are not fun emotions, they are emotions. She has come so far from where she was and one day at a time there is gratefully a long road of recovery ahead. I just read the autobiography of knuckleballer RA Dickey, two quotes from the book fit here with the first by Longfellow "Go forth to meet the shadowy Future without fear and with a manly heart." and by Dickey "One of the enduring challenges of living on this side of eternity: how to live fully in the pain of the moment as well as the joy of the moment." Joy is working to stay in the moment and also picturing the victory of recovery. There is a lot inside of me right now, lots of gratitude for such awesome friends and family, trust in the Loving God, with some fear.

June 7, 2012 by Joy Pentz: Things are still going well. The ICU doctor wants to be paged when the oncologist is here to discuss getting out of ICU. Last night Elise was quite awake. I told her I was so sorry she was going through all this. I couldn't understand what she mouthed in response, so I asked her to write it. She wrote, "It isn't you're fault." Maybe that was her form of apology for telling me she was angry with me. I had to smile when I saw her mistake writing you're instead of your. One of her friends said back in Feb she knew Elise was better after her surgery when she corrected someone's comment on Facebook, and told him the correct word was you're, not your. If you're (not your) that person, you can now give Elise a hard time about that. We are really happy with Elise getting her emotions back. Last night I asked if she was scared, and she nodded yes. I told her about the vaccine made with her tumor cells and her blood, and she raised her eyebrows and smiled. So far we have seen angry, scared and depressed, so hopefully forgiving, courageous and jubilant are not far behind.

Last night Elise was awake enough to say yes when I asked her if she wanted me to read her Caring Bridge messages to her. I didn't know if she was ever going to ask me to stop. She closed her eyes a few times, and I asked if she wanted me to keep reading, and she kept saying yes. About the time my voice was giving out, she fell asleep. She loved hearing your messages, so please keep them coming. Marty and I love reading them too. Some of you have said you like reading the guest book as well.

I washed and braided Elise's hair today, which I love to do. I hated to see so much of it coming out so easily. I have to admit it is more than normal. I collected about a fist full. Good thing she has lots more where that came from. It is possible that the hair may not grow back where the radiation is entering her head, but her hair is so thick, it will cover it. Anyway, hair is way down on the list of issues right now.

I asked the Occupational Therapist about her dropped left foot, because I am concerned about her being able to walk. She said a brace can be made to keep her foot in a neutral position so she can walk even if she does not regain use of those ankle muscles. I read advice from another parent going through this, and they said to just keep two thoughts in your mind. 1. What must be done to get through today, and 2. Victory. That has been very helpful because it is hard to imagine going from today to victory without worrying about the "what ifs." I picture victory as Elise standing before an audience talking about her victory over addiction and brain cancer as a motivational speaker, making her audience laugh and staying after for a book signing. Elise's friends knew something was wrong with her when she stopped trying to make people laugh. She loves to do that and to write. She expressed fear about being capable of finishing college after her surgery, so I told her not to worry, she could be a motivational writer and speaker, and she liked that.

From: Pentz, Marty

Sent: Friday, June 08, 2012 3:27 AM With today's post I am also placing a reminder of the brain tumor walk tomorrow. I along with other hospital staff members are going to participate in a 5K walk/run in honor of Elise Pentz. I have provided a link below for anyone that would like to join us. The online registration is $20. It will be $25 day of event. Feel free to make a donation in her honor if you are not able to attend. Please forward to anyone I may have left out. HEAD FOR THE CURE. A fun and family oriented 5K walk/run to raise awareness and research funding for the American Brain Tumor Association. www.braincure.org West Park 2700 W. 116th Street Hours: REGISTRATION 730am; Event Start 9am Team Name: TEAM PENTZ

0251 hours. Sleepy tonight, not quite enough sleep. Elise is sleeping quietly at the moment. Something was different when I came in her room tonight and then I noticed the ventilator machine was gone. She has been breathing on her own since Monday 7pm, with some oxygen. Just less than 4 weeks ago I thought she was gone, now she can communicate with us and has some emotional access. Prior to admission she had no short-term memory and now she remembers nurses day to day. She has limited ability to use her left side to date, but she can move it at will a little. When I look ahead I see an arduous journey, but when addressed right now and day by day it looks glorious. Elise and all her family and friends have a great support system, headed by God. With the added Love from God we have love in spades.

June 8, 2012 by Joy Pentz: I just got my daily dose of energy and inspiration---sunshine and reading your messages on Caring Bridge. Progress note for today: Since yesterday afternoon Elise has answered no when we ask her if she is seeing double! She had been seeing double since late March. The miracles continue. Please keep praying.

My mom may have something in common with Elise soon, due to my sister, Doreen, watching a TV show in which the opposition in a court trial opposed the testimony of a person with Alzheimer's. It turns out the person had NPH, Normal Pressure Hydrocephalous. It is caused by too much spinal fluid in the brain causing pressure on brain tissue. There is an explanation of why it is called normal pressure, but...like I said at the end of all my book reports in elementary school, if you want to know what happens, read the book. NPH can cause memory issues, gait problems and urinary incontinence.

When Doreen heard those symptoms, she insisted my dad take my mom to a neurologist to see if that is what she has, and went with him to insist the doctor look for NPH. The neurologist said her scan shows she does. The next step is to drain 30 ml of spinal fluid and see how my mom walks. If her gait improves, they will do a permanent shunt to regulate the pressure on her brain tissue. The neurologist said she does not have Alzheimer's, which they thought she had the last 7 years. NPH is the good news. Frontotemporal Dementia (FTD) is the bad news. (Hmm, FTD. Should I stop sending her flowers for Mother's Day?) It is similar to Alzheimer's but occurs in a different part of the brain, and involves the buildup of three proteins. The neurologist gave her a different Alzheimer's drug to try to treat for the FTD. Even if my mom's memory does not improve, if the walking and urinary incontinence can be solved, my dad will have a much easier time as her caregiver. FTD evidently does not cause the change in personality common in Alzheimer's, so that's why my mom has remained as sweet as she has always been. If anyone saw the same show (one person thought it might be "The Good Wife"), let me know. I would like to watch it. Yay for Doreen for not being afraid to look silly in front of Dad or the neurologist.

I am the oldest of this generation on this side of the family, so my sisters and cousins have probably all been anxiously awaiting to see if I am going to get Alzheimer's. My uncles and grandmother were all thought to have it. Before you get too excited, if it was FTD, unfortunately that is also often hereditary. BTW, I think my memory is OK so far for my age. This ties back to Elise, so I didn't veer way off topic. When I asked Elise after her nap if she remembered about my mom getting a shunt, she nodded yes. She sometimes nods no to memory questions, so I think she really did remember.

Elise just got back from radiation. The anesthesiologist said he had to give her 3X the dosage of yesterday because she is so much more alert! That's really good to know because she is still withdrawing from the Fentanyl drip by taking morphine, and she looks pretty spaced out at times. I am comforted that she is not trying to take advantage of the morphine to get high because she sometimes says she doesn't need it, and the time between doses is sometimes longer. Hope I am not boring you with details, but I thought the NPH info might be helpful to others, since it is often misdiagnosed as Parkinson's or Alzheimer's, and the sooner you can treat it the better chance the problems can be corrected.

June 8, 2012 by Joy Pentz: Elise was moved to a regular room today. Progress.

From: Pentz, Marty

Sent: Friday, June 08, 2012 9:45 PM 2124 hours. Elise was moved to a regular oncology room this afternoon. This is wonderful and scary at the same time. She is not monitored as much. Her double vision has stopped and most other symptoms are decreasing as well. Joy and Drew are staying with her tonight and I am actually at home. Not sure what it will be like to sleep in my bed. Seeing the Spirit in most of life is helping me to do this day by day, but I have not been able to feel this way as much as I would like. Must mean there is still work for me to do. Loving Elise is a wonderful experience as I focus on this. It is hard to see her struggle and suffer. She says she is feeling "ok" most of the time, but to see her lying there unable to care for herself is hard. As she progresses I know this will get better and staying present makes this possible daily. Please keep the love and prayers coming.

June 9, 2012 by Joy Pentz

The nurses on the oncology floor are just as caring and competent as the nurses in ICU. They have fewer opportunities to suction the lungs through the trach opening, however, and seem afraid to go too deep. It is awful to see and listen to the procedure. Elise has had two extended episodes of gurgling with every breath. I'm not sure she would be able to hit the nurse button to call for help. She didn't have any of these episodes in ICU. I'm so glad I was here to get help. I am sleeping on a cot next to Elise's bed, and the other amenities in this room like a shower and fridge are great. No new developments to report.

From: Pentz, Marty: Sent Saturday, June 09, 2012 8:52 PM 2041 hours. Elise continues to improve daily, she has been awake more today than she has been. She is doing well in her new room. She has radiation until the 29th of June so will probably be in this room until then. The current plan is for her to go to inpatient rehab after that. Watching the tenderness of Joy's love for Elise has been a blessing. Watching how she lovingly washes her hair is so cool. Went on a fundraising walk called Head for the Cure raising money for brain tumor research. Some friends from work found this walk and it was great to do this with them and Roger. You guys are the best. It felt good to do some rather mundane chores today. Mowed the grass, cleaned the kitchen some and went through 4 weeks of mail, threw away most of it. Today has been a good day.

June 10, 2012 by Joy Pentz. The nurse just told me Elise was done with her chemo; it was ordered for 26 days. I told her, no, she is supposed to take it for 42 days, every day. She said she would check with the pharmacist. All I know is she is going to get her dose somehow. What do people do who don't have family to watch over them? Earlier today, one of the nurses who cared for Elise yesterday, called the doctor on her own initiative, and asked if he could order a speech valve so Elise could speak with the trach. She just felt it must be very difficult for a 20 year old not to be able to speak. She was not able to make any sounds with the speech valve, and her breathing was labored with it. The way it works is that air goes in through the trach, but then the valve closes, so the air is forced to go over the vocal cords as it is exhaled through the nose and mouth. It is frustrating not to be able to speak with a doctor about the cause, but I learned from the internet that there are several causes and solutions. The nurse just got the doctor to extend the chemo order, so she will not miss her dose tonight. I am very happy being at the hospital with Elise, and feel honored to be a part of her healing team. As always, your messages are so encouraging. Thanks!

From: Pentz, Marty. Sent: Sunday, June 10, 2012 9:57 PM 2137 hours. Another day of holding steady. Respiratory therapy put a talking gizmo on her trach and Elise was unable to use it at this point due to some issue above her trach in her throat or it could be she is just too tired. Joy found an article about using modified trach talking tubes where it would take less air to be able to talk. Elise is breathing fine on her own with just a little bit ...of oxygen, but not able to talk yet. We will discuss these and a few other things with the doctors tomorrow. Her not being able talk yet was disappointing, but today she is breathing well, knows all that have come to see her and no double vision. Elise had a number of friends visit today as well as my sister Kaye. It was great fun singing to Elise with Joy and the two Matt's from Trinity that came to sing with us today. Still focusing on daily joys, getting through today with as much peace as possible with my eyes on Victory and Elise having a life this side of eternity. Marty

June 11, 2012 by Joy Pentz

Elise wrote, "I'm just hungry for waffles or pancakes." She just needs to learn to control the movements necessary to swallow and speak. She will have a swallow test soon. Your messages are so empowering, so please keep them coming. Thanks, Joy

From: Pentz, Marty: Sent Monday, June 11, 2012 10:26 PM 2209 hours. Elise was working hard to talk with her trach talking gizmo, I like this word, but she appears to be just tired at this point. She struggles to have energy to help with the physical therapy and occupational therapy as well. Will discuss with the Drs. about ways to boost her energy for the short term so she can work harder on re-learning to use her body, brain and all its various parts. Moving to a new floor has taken some getting used to. I had the rhythm of the ICU down. After talking with the nurses and getting some things discussed I think we have this new floor to Elise's benefit as well. It is hard for me to see her not being able to talk, but I know she will talk before long. I see her progress as incremental at times, which is still progress and people that do not see her daily see the changes as big. That perspective is good for me. Interestingly through all of this my Love and Faith in God is stronger now than prior to this tumor stuff beginning. Time to pray and meditate, good night.

June 12, 2012 by Joy Pentz

Today started out with a thumbs up when I asked Elise how she was doing. It had been a so-so motion of her hand. She was able to wiggle her left foot and squeeze with her left hand. She sat on the side of the bed supporting herself with her hands and stood at the side of the bed with the support of the physical therapist. All this is so encouraging.

Elise had three items which added to her comfort today. She got a waffle air mattress. It's not exactly what she had in mind when she wrote that she wanted waffles, but it is supposed to prevent pressure sores. I wonder why no one thought of that before. She also got a heater to warm up the air used to humidify the oxygen going into her trach. This should thin her secretions, allowing her to cough them up herself rather than be suctioned, and should make it easier for her to breathe with the speech valve. Suctioning really sucks---she gags and coughs like a seal barking. Marty always leaves the room. I finally got an explanation of exactly how the process works to come off the trach. It starts with the speech valve which allows air in through the trach, but closes off after the inhale to force the exhale out the nose and mouth. After she is able to breathe well with the speech valve, it is replaced by a plug. When she can inhale and exhale comfortably with the plug, the trach can be removed.

The third thing for comfort allowed her to have her hair shampooed with real shampoo and water instead of no rinse foam. One of Elise's friends who is a nurse told me about a devise which facilitates shampooing. It is a sheet of plastic with an inflatable ring around it to hold the water. There is a drain hole with a tube that is placed in a bucket. Marty and I washed Elise's hair, and she seemed to enjoy it. Marty washed a little too vigorously, and now she has a huge knot about 3" in diameter we will try to untangle with No More Tangles tomorrow. I did my best, but it is a monster knot. It makes me wonder how much more hair Marty would have today if he had washed his own hair less vigorously over the years.

From: Pentz, Marty. Sent: Tuesday, June 12, 2012 9:45 PM 2120 hours. This has been a more than a good day. Elise was able to move her left toes when asked and squeeze with her left hand as well. She has not been able to use her left side much at all for months. She was also able, with help, to stand three times and to sit at the edge of the bed for ten minutes. She threw a ball to me when asked. I helped Joy to wash her hair as well. She is improving daily. This day of progress was the balm for my sanity. All her therapy is progressing. Sometimes my love for God is not as strong as I would like it to be. God's love for all of us, in this case my daughter Elise, knows no bounds. She is being healed

June 13, 2012 by Joy Pentz

Today Elise was able to chew and swallow ice chips. She still has not been able to vocalize with the speech valve. Tomorrow, the speech therapist with the most expertise on trachs will try to figure out what the problem is. I worked for a long time on the knot in Elise's hair with detangler, but I barely made a dent. She is losing more and more hair, so I should probably just wait for it to fall out. I have been saving all the hair that falls out, and have quite a pile of it. I'm not sure what I will do with it yet.

Elise wrote some more. We asked her to write her brother's and sister's names, which she did easily. Then we asked her to write her boyfriend's name, and she hesitated and then wrote Basil. When we asked her to point to her boyfriend, she pointed to Drew. When we asked her to point to Drew, she pointed to him. When we asked how old she was she wrote 12. She did like a boy named Basil when she was not much older than 12. This confusion was a bit discouraging to me, but when we told her she was 20, she was able to write the number.

I just have to believe that through therapy she will recoup any brain damage the tumor has done. She is still on morphine, meds to prevent seizures, chemo and radiation, etc., so it should not be so surprising she has some confusion, especially considering she is on the verge of sleep most of the time. I have to remember the advice of just getting through today and picturing victory. It is the uncertainty and the process of reaching victory that is scary to me. I am very tired because I wake up every two hours when the nurses reposition Elise and rotate her boot. She has a special boot to hold her foot in neutral to correct drop foot. It is supposed to be put on the other foot every two hours. When I am tired, it is harder to remain cheerful and positive. I will try earplugs tonight. I am going to go to bed now and try to read something uplifting. Please keep praying. Thank you.

> *Comment from Joy, February 18, 2018: When it was time for Elise's radiation, they would leave her in her bed and wheel her away. When they took her bed out of the room, it was easier for me to gather her lost hair from the floor. One day, the woman who mopped the floor saw me collecting the hair, and asked me what I was doing. When I told her I just wanted her hair, but I didn't know what I would do with it, the look on her face was so sympathetic. After that, whenever she cleaned Elise's room, I would later find a Ziploc bag filled with Elise's hair. I still have Elise's hair, but have not done anything with it.*
>
> *The kindness of all the staff at St. Vincent Hospital was remarkable. The woman who cleaned the room when Elise was in ICU told me she was praying for Elise every day.*

The CNAs and Nurses were all wonderful as well. Many prayed for Elise, and showered us with acts of kindness. One ICU nurse would always bring me two servings of orange juice during her shift. If I was asleep on the couch, I would find the juice on the end table when I awoke. After Elise moved to the cancer floor, she periodically came to visit on her breaks to see how Elise was doing. I was so touched, not only by her visits, but also that she would bring along two servings of orange juice for me. This was the same nurse who first suggested the speaking valve for Elise. Months later, a friend told me she asked one of the ICU nurses, what was the next step for Elise, and the nurse just sadly shook her head. A few years later, when I took Elise to a CVS Minute Clinic for a sore throat, the nurse practitioner remembered us from the St. Vincent ICU. When I said, "I bet you are surprised to see is Elise still alive," she admitted she was.

After Elise had finished all her treatment, and we were no longer in crisis mode, Marty and I found we needed help to deal with the traumatic experience we had gone through, and the stress we were still feeling. We each went to a therapist for a few sessions for EMDR, Eye Movement Desensitization and Reprocessing, which is used for treating PTSD, Post-Traumatic Stress Disorder. Although the technique can also be done with musical tones or tapping, the original acronym has stuck. Our EMDR therapist used musical tones while having us reprocess the events, as she guided our thoughts to more pleasant ones. I used the kind acts of the St. Vincent staff to reprocess the traumatic events. I find that when I recall these events, the feeling of fear has been replaced with a feeling of pleasantness.

After we got our dog, Lucy, in December of 2013, Marty found that when he would get on the floor to play with her, it triggered the trauma of coming home and seeing Elise on an air mattress on the floor struggling to breathe. That was the event that initiated the ambulance ride which resulted in Elise going on life support. By that time, Elise had drop foot, and could no longer walk or climb stairs to go to her bedroom, so she slept on an air mattress on the living room floor. Ever since EMDR, Marty is able to get on the floor to play with Lucy; she is too big to sit on your lap. Now playing with Lucy is one of the most comforting things Marty does for himself.

From: Pentz, Marty. Sent: Wednesday, June 13, 2012 9:07 PM 2056 hours. Elise was able to swallow a few ice chips today, but still no talking, but that will come. She clearly understands what is being said and what is going on, but her body will not follow directions yet. She has progressed enough that I will be going back to work next Monday and will be on intermittent FMLA to use when needed. She will be in St. Vincent's about two more weeks until radiation is complete and then inpatient rehab for unknown length of time. When she is finally home I will need to be present more again for rehab and appointments. I am ready to return to work, but already miss being there as much as I have been. I also finished cleaning the house today, and our new vacuum cleaner works wonders. Emily gave me a wonderful father's day gift today, a coffee mug with Happy Father's day on one side with a picture of Emily, Elise and me, and on the other side it says, "World's Greatest Dad," with a picture of Daniel, Emily and me. I cried when I opened the gift today, it was needed today. There is so much love in my life, God, Joy Elise, Emily, Daniel

June 14, 2012 by Joy Pentz: Today Elise knew Drew. He asked where she wanted to go when she gets out and she wrote Noodles and Co. She wrote X-mas when he asked if she remembered their anniversary, and she wrote I love you with a smiley face. She was able to tolerate the speech valve for 3 periods of 10 minutes with her heart rate and breathing OK, but she is still not able to vocalize. She will have an ENT consult. She was not able to support herself sitting on the side of the bed. She was so sleepy she had trouble even holding her head up. I appreciate everyone's concern about me. I am taking care of myself. I am eating well. I walk outside while Elise is in radiation. I am getting to bed earlier and using earplugs to sleep better. I am going to try using an eye mask also to block the light. I am making a gratitude list most days, and it lifts my spirits. I know if I knew everything would turn out ok, I would not have any problem going through this. I actually love spending this time nurturing Elise. It is fear that makes it difficult. I guess that goes back to getting through today and picturing victory. I need to find happiness and contentment in the little things of each day. Please keep praying and writing. It helps so much.

From: Pentz, Marty. Sent: Thursday, June 14, 2012 6:12 PM 1752 hours. Home early today. Elise continues to work hard at speaking and is struggling with physical therapy. When I remember she was completely sedated and I thought she might die just four weeks ago, she is doing very well. Watching headlines on the Tonight Show and it is so good to laugh and to be able to as well. I came across two quotes that touched me today: "I walk slowly, but I never walk backward." – Abraham Lincoln and "Some of the greatest battles will be fought within the silent chambers of your own soul." -Ezra Taft Benson. This last one has been my thinking for some 30 years now. As with Lincoln, with God all is forward, even when it does not appear so.

June 15, 2012 by Joy Pentz

I am so happy today. We had the ENT consult. The doctor looked at Elise's vocal cords in action with a probe inserted through her nose. She said they are both moving and touching each other as they should, though the left one is a bit sluggish. She believed it is just a matter of Elise building up her strength again. This was really good news. The fear was they could have been damaged or paralyzed by intubation. The other great news is that Elise is able to move her left side so much more than we have seen. While laying down, she is able to press her foot against the physical therapist's hand, roll her leg inward and out, press down on the therapist's fingers under her knees. While sitting on the side of the bed, she can kick her leg out repeatedly. We were all clapping at her accomplishments.

From: Pentz, Marty.   Sent: Friday, June 15, 2012 8:55 PM 2022 hours. 4 weeks ago Elise was not able to move any of her left side, but today during physical therapy she was sitting on the edge of the bed, with support, and was able to move her left leg by herself and her left arm some. She is working hard and improving daily. God is good. Discussing her effort with her oncologist she was impressed. She stated that with all that is going on with Elise her effort is like a marathon to us. At times this has been an immensely scary journey, but Elise's effort, courage and desire to live and be better has been encouraging. The love and support and prayers that Elise, Joy and I have been receiving is priceless as well. I have been thinking about this quote today: "I want to know God's thoughts; the rest are details." Einstein. Another quote by Einstein describes some of my recent thoughts and experiences. "The most beautiful thing we can experience is the mysterious. It is the source of all true art and all science. He to whom this emotion is a stranger, who can no longer pause to wonder and stand rapt in awe, is as good as dead: his eyes are closed." Many times in the past 6 months I have stood "rapt in awe" at the love in our lives and the experience of God's presence I have often felt lately.

June 16, 2012 by Joy Pentz: I always read your messages before I post an update, and they are so inspiring. Thanks so much for all your support. Elise is doing well right now, but we had a scare last night. The doctor ordered breathing treatment 3X/day to help her lungs relax and release her secretions. On the third treatment her heart rate rose to the high 130s and stayed there. The Rapid Response Team was called, and they attached some monitors, but once they figured out it must be the albuterol, they left. Her oxygen was fine, and she didn't look uncomfortable, just some jitteriness, hot, red face and heavy breathing. Her heart rate was still in the 120s in the morning, and it is now 89. Her normal heart rate has been around 50. The doctor changed the medication to something that does not have cardiac side effects. They don't use it first because it is more expensive. I was given albuterol for pre-term labor when I was pregnant with Elise, and had to be on complete bed rest with two months to go. They took me off after a month because at that point the risk of lung problems was lower than the risk of continued albuterol, and she was born within 24 hours. Who knows, maybe Elise developed a sensitivity in utero?

In the category of TMI, Elise's urine looks like grape juice, only with thick sediment. We are waiting for lab results. She finally responded to the bowel protocol today. Yay! Marty always says he never thought he'd be talking about this in regard to his 20 year old daughter, but it is important. Elise was upgraded from her waffle mattress to an Envision bed, which is even better for pressure redistribution. She has not had any pressure sores, but one of the nurses suggested it. We can take the waffle mattress and pump home with us. When she comes home, maybe we will sit on it to eat waffles.

I did my normal Saturday morning activities, and it was great to take care of myself in that way. When I came back, Elise was watching a movie, and quite engrossed, which is a good thing. Marty did her physical therapy, and I will do a second session later. I am not going to put on the speech valve until her heart rate returns to normal. Right now Marty is getting my favorite sandwich for me, grilled portabella mushroom. He is so nurturing to me.

This paragraph is for everyone who expressed concern about my taking care of myself. I will go to bed early tonight because I didn't get much sleep last night due to the heart rate incident until 1:00 am and a noisy nurse at 5:30 am. Elise's recovery is a miracle, and I am so happy you are enjoying sharing it with us. Thank you for your continued prayer as well.

From: Pentz, Marty. Sent: Saturday, June 16, 2012 6:48 PM 1835 hours. Elise was awake for much of the day today. She did not want to interact much, but did watch some TV and visited with three friends for about an hour or so. Did her physical therapy with her and she was able to help move her left side some; progress is small but ongoing. She is having some urinary issues and the Dr. will be in soon. She has done very well with all the poking and prodding since the 12th of May, this trip to the hospital. Two more weeks of radiation and then rehab hospital. It is great to see her progress daily, but I struggled some today with her difficulty. Prayer and meditation helped a lot and the visit from Grace, the priest, helped as well. I like her and Tom's prayers. They are the clergy where Elise and I sing at church. Joy's cousin is visiting today and that has been good for her. Going back to work on Monday and I will find out then if I am ready. Has been a good day. From Yoda "Truly wonderful the mind of a child is." Elise's mind appears to be working well, just need to get it re-connected to the rest of her body.

From: Pentz, Marty. Sent: Sunday, June 17, 2012 9:29 PM 2113 hours. Elise slept for much of radiation and fever today. She was simply worn out. Fever was gone later in the day. I used to run and prior to hurting my knee I wanted to run in a mini marathon or marathon someday. I am running the marathon now. Two more weeks of radiation and about 8 days or so of chemo. Once off of the treatment she will have more energy to work hard on all the different types of therapy she is having. I was discussing with a group of friends tonight the privilege of being part of a fellowship. Many felt undeserving of the mercy they have received. I look at this a little differently. As children of a loving God, we are all worthy of love, miracles, and a life of useful service. This is not due to anything we have done or not done, but to my belief in who and what God is. I am back to work tomorrow. We march on.

Jun 17, 2012 11:05pm by Joy Pentz

My day started out magnificently. The doctor gave me a good lab report about Elise's urine. I had been told last night that it showed she had kidney damage because there were casts in her urine. He said it was probably from one of her meds, but it could be cancer. We had wonderful visits with friends and family. I went home to do some chores and played violin while I was there. It was so uplifting to make music again. Even though Elise is suffering because of her treatment, she is so much better. I was elated the speculation about cancer in her kidneys was not accurate. If only a doctor would walk in and tell us Elise's brain tumor was misdiagnosed!

June 19, 2012 by Joy Pentz: At least 2 victories to announce today. Elise smiled 3 times without prompting today. She has refused to try to speak lately after a few failed attempts. I asked if she would try to speak if no one was in the room. She said yes, so I left. When I came back I asked if she tried to speak, and she said no. When I said, "So you lied?" she smiled and nodded yes. I asked why she didn't want to speak and she shrugged her shoulder, so I asked her to say that again louder. She shrugged her shoulder a little more forcefully and smiled.

I asked if she remembered when I took her to see David Sedaris, and she nodded yes. I reminded her that after she found out how much the tickets cost, she was surprised I paid that much. Then on the way home she said I was a good person. I asked if she thought I was a bad person before, and she said no, just annoying. Then she hurried to tell me I was still annoying, but a good person. She smiled when I reminded her of what she said. It was so wonderful to see those genuine smiles.

The other victory later in the day was Elise finally tried to vocalize, and was able to voice "ahhh" with the speech valve. She repeated for the nurse, then for Marty and later for the speech therapist. She won't try to say anything else, but the nurse told her she would not be back until Tues, and she had to be able to say her name, Lauren, by then. Maybe she finally tried again because she felt guilty for lying to me. Yesterday Elise was able to sit on the edge of the bed for 15 minutes with the physical therapist letting go of her occasionally for short periods. She was asked to kick her left leg out 10 times, and she was able to do it. From what we have been told, it is quite amazing to be able to sit by herself after so many weeks of lying in bed. I washed Elise's hair again with the special inflatable basin that drains. I poured the conditioner on her big knot, but it's still just as big. I'll keep working on it. If I can't ever untangle it, she might start a new hairstyle trend or we can cut it off when her hair gets longer. Please keep your prayers and messages coming. We are very grateful.

From: Pentz, Marty: Sent Monday, June 18, 2012 8:55 PM   Missed Elise and Joy while I worked today, but it felt good to be there. Elise is so tired. She was able to wear the speaking valve for over two hours today without breathing problems, but will not attempt to talk with us. She has tried with the speech therapist so maybe she will tomorrow. During physical therapy today she was able to sit on the edge of the bed for about 15 minutes and three times was able to hold herself there for 10-15 seconds or so. First time she was able to hold herself up. When progress is slow I need to remember that on May 14th she was not expected to live from hours to days. A couple of quotes for today that remind me we need to get Elise to laugh more: "The art of medicine consists in amusing the patient while nature cures the disease." Voltaire. Another quote for faith "The greatest mistake in the treatment of diseases is that there are physicians for the body and physicians for the soul, although the two cannot be separated." ~Plato We keep praying while the medical folks do their thing

From: Pentz, Marty. Sent: Tuesday, June 19, 2012 10:23 PM. Elise had a good work day today. She was able to make sounds through her trach speaking valve for the first time. Her physical therapy went well. She can move her left leg, foot and her fingers in therapy and works hard at it. She has never been without the use of her right side, but these sides are worked as well. We are so blessed with this progress. Joy reported that she smiled a few times without prompting; she will smile when asked. I was asked a few days ago by my brother Pat how I saw the Book of Job from the Bible in relation to Elise's brain tumor/cancer. I meet with a small group of men two times per month and we discuss various books, usually based on spirituality or religion. Lately we have been studying the spiritual exercises of St. Ignatius Jesuits. With Pat's question I asked to have Job added to our discussion. After a re-reading of the chapter and our discussion earlier this evening, Pat, here is my answer. From all the reading I have done it seems clear to me that people throughout time have been trying to make sense of the good and bad that happens to people. The first section of Job makes the argument that God is testing Job and/or the Job has sinned in some way. This sin approach is the tact taken by those around Job. When God finally talks near the end He does not appear to even address the Satan or sin issue. He talks about the Wonder and Awe of Creation. I believe God is saying that I created all this wonder so why would I mess with you. The Book of Job is saying to me that God does not create brain tumors in beautiful 19 year old young women like Elise. He does give me access to the strength, love and prayers of others to discern from the various courses of action which ones to take. My reasoning can take me a long way - all the modern medicine being applied to Elise's care, but it is my Faith and Faith alone that I leap to the belief she will be ok and have a good life on this side of eternity. If the other side of eternity is reached by her before her mother or me, we will see her again.

June 20, 2012 by Joy Pentz: Thanks to Andy and her experience as a mom of four daughters, we got Elise's knot out with canola oil, a paper clip and a hair pick. One small, but important victory because it was uncomfortable for Elise to lay on the knot. Hopefully it won't be uncomfortable for her when the broken paper clip shows up. When I opened up the paperclip, it broke so I recruited Marty to help me with the other half. Before he could start using his half of the paper clip, it fell, bounced on the pillow and disappeared. I told Marty if he didn't want to help he should have just said so. He said if he didn't want to help he wouldn't be standing there. That's when I found the hair pick. He has yet to take responsibility for the monstrosity he created. I just think it's funny because all I did was ask him to lift Elise's head up, and he washed it at the same time and remarked that I was hardly washing her hair when he saw how gently I did it.

Elise woke up very depressed today. The only thing she wanted to do is listen to your messages on Caring Bridge. I read them until my voice gave out, and then I read some more later on. She was still quite depressed, but it helped. In one of the messages, Maggie wrote about YouTube clips of laughing babies. I played them for Elise, but she didn't crack a smile. We'll try again tomorrow. They always cheer me up. I am reading a book called "The Noticer" by Andy Andrews (thanks Kathi). It is uplifting, so I thought Elise might like it. I put it in her hands, and she was able to read and turn the pages, but I don't think she got too far because she kept nodding off. One of the meds Elise is on to prevent seizures, Keppra, has a side effect of depression. None of the EEGs showed she has had seizures, so she will come off of that med after radiation is over. Then her Cymbalta should be able to do its job better.

I kept suggesting different things Elise could do, but none of them interested her. She finally said she wanted to eat. I was so happy she wanted to do something. I told her she had to use the speech valve to get to eat, so she agreed to put it on. She said hi. Then she said, "My name is Elise Pentz," with prompting. Her voice is getting stronger and louder. She is building up her throat muscles and will soon be able to eat. A very aggressive physical therapist worked with Elise today. She had her sitting on the bed for a long time, and she was able to balance herself for several minutes. She stood her up by the bed, and told me Elise practically stood up by herself. Then transport came to take her to radiation. The therapist said she would have tried walking if we had more time. Elise is now able to move her left arm a bit, so it's just a matter of time and strengthening her muscles, and she'll be back to her normal self.

The speech therapist went through some exercises with her to see how she was processing. She was able to answer the questions and repeat back long sentences. She spoke by putting her finger on her trach because the inner cannula was changed, and it is not compatible with her speech valve. That will be fixed tomorrow. She was able to breathe so well with the valve, I am going to ask the lung doctor if he will order a plug for the trach so she can get used to breathing just through her nose and mouth. The speech therapist said she can try her on soft foods like pudding tomorrow. I asked the radiologist if he could order pet therapy, and they came to her room twice while she was still in radiation. Hopefully she will be in her room when they come tomorrow. All this progress is truly amazing and miraculous. Thanks for all your prayers and messages. They mean a lot to us.

From: Pentz, Marty. Sent: Wednesday, June 20, 2012 8:08 PM. Amazing progress today. During physical therapy Elise was able to stand up with help and sit at the side of the bed on her own for brief periods of time. During OT she also was able to move her left arm on her own as well. Then later during speech therapy she said, "Hi Dad," and was able to repeat back a number of sentences from the therapist. It was great to hear her voice. I was glad I was at work when earlier today she was taking her speaking valve off and pulled the trach out. They quickly put another one in. It is such a blessing to watch her get better and to love her so. Joy is such an amazing mom. I have been reading the journals of Thomas Merton and in his entry for January 29th 1966 he states the following: "What matters is to love, to be in one place in silence, if necessary in suffering, sickness, tribulation, and not try to be anybody outwardly." I see this in Joy, she is simply being Elise's mom. I love her so.

June 21, 2012 by Joy Pentz: Great news. Elise has had a cap on her trach for about 6 hours with no effect on her heart rate or blood oxygen level. This means she can breathe fine through her mouth and nose, so she should get the trach out in a couple of days. She is very reluctant to speak, and she said she is scared she won't be able to speak. It is a little difficult because the trach is smaller than the hole the surgeon made, so air is escaping. Once her trach is removed, the hole can heal and she will be able to speak much more easily, especially as those muscles get stronger. Elise had occupational therapy, pet therapy and physical therapy today. The dogs really cheered her up. She is sitting better, but the PT was right after radiation/anesthesia so she was not too steady on her feet. She tried to take a step sideways with her right foot, but her left knee buckled, so the therapist laid her back down and did some bed exercises.

We watched a video someone sent showing children and employees at a children's hospital singing and dancing to a Kelly Clarkson's song, "What doesn't kill you makes you stronger". Elise liked it better than the baby videos, and said it cheered her up. Thanks JoAnn. Elise was also cheered up by reading the Caring Bridge messages. Thank you everyone. I read some, and then she read some herself, but reading makes her fall asleep. Elise seems to get more depressed every day. I assure her that will get better, and explained that taking her off the seizure meds next week should help a lot. She said she is not scared she won't live; she is scared she will live. One thing she is concerned about is her intelligence. I explained that the location of the tumor affected her mathematical functioning. The rest of her intelligence has been spared. I spoke with her in Spanish to help her see that she hasn't lost it. She criticized my Spanish, so she recognizes the language well enough to know I'm rusty.

Elise finishes radiation and chemo next Friday, and I know she will do so much better. For one thing she can't have any nutrition after midnight because of the anesthesia for radiation. Then she can't have any nutrition 2 hours before and after chemo. They upped her calories, but she is really lacking energy. Today I met a 93 year old woman. I asked what her secret was to stay so healthy. She said she works 5 hours a day at a nursery, and it keeps her active, and she gets and gives love to the children. She has been doing it for 20 years. Her 2-1/2 year old great granddaughter tells her when it is time to go to work because she taught her where the hands on the clock should be. She lost part of a lung to cancer 7 years ago, but she is able to walk to work down the street. It cheered me up to talk to her. It is hard to stay cheerful around someone who is so depressed.

> *Comment by Marty, January 18, 2018: Elise being afraid to live without knowing how well she will function is much like how I felt in my late 20's in early recovery. I started to wake up emotionally, realizing I did not know how to be a true partner. It was frightening, but also a stepping stone into a life worth living. One of my hopes is that Elise sees the possible in her struggle forward. This quote says succinctly what I wordily just said, "If there is no struggle, there is no progress." Frederick Douglass*

From: Pentz, Marty. Sent: Thursday, June 21, 2012 8:50 PM. Elise continues to improve physically daily. They stood her up again and she is talking more. She said, "Hi Dad," when I came in this evening. She is seriously struggling with depression. When Joy talked to her more Elise told her she is fearful she will not be smart anymore. It is heart wrenching to see her so depressed. When they brought the pet therapy dogs today she was cheered lot. We are apparently and joyfully getting a dog when she comes home. As she keeps improving daily I believe she will also get better emotionally. I have some fear as well of how Elise will be as living with cancer. My hope is for her to have a chance at a full life with some joy and contentment.

She has a plug valve on her trach and she was still able to breathe well and talk more. This will be taken off for tonight and put back on in the morning. My understanding of the plan is for her to be able to do well with the plug in for 24 or 48 hours and then probably take the trach out. She is progressing in so many ways so fast. My heart and soul are filled with peace when I see the progress made. Today has been a good day in most ways. Goodnight all.

From: Pentz, Marty: Sent Friday, June 22, 2012 10:48 PM. 2221 hours. This has been a long and fruitful week for our family. Emily is getting closer to having her baby across the pond. Elise has been progressing daily and getting closer to the end of this phase of treatment. She may get the trach out tomorrow. It has been good for me to be back at work, even with missing being at the hospital. Elise can talk fairly well, but will not do it much yet. She was able to stand again today, but not take a step as her left leg is not strong enough yet. Joy found some scripts for guided imagery for cancer patients. I will be recording these tomorrow and Sunday as well as designing my own or adding to the ones from on-line. I have found these kind of recordings quite helpful in my own life. We keep praying and moving along. I came across this poem and I want to share it with all of you. What Cancer Cannot Do Cancer is so limited.... It cannot cripple love. It cannot shatter hope. It cannot corrode faith. It cannot eat away peace. It cannot destroy confidence. It cannot kill friendship. It cannot shut out memories. It cannot silence courage. It cannot reduce eternal life. It cannot quench the Spirit. Author Unknown

June 23, 2012 by Joy Pentz. This journey certainly is not a straight line, but it's still going up. Elise's heart rate started going up last evening and she felt bad. She woke up with what seems to be a cold/sore throat. The doctor ordered some numbing spray for her throat, but we haven't gotten it yet. Last night when she ran out of the food to go in her tube, there were no more cans of 2 calorie goop for her. Today I learned the order had been cancelled accidently. The doctor on call was "uncomfortable" ordering something, and it was close to time for the next doctor's shift, so she passed the buck. Elise went four hours without food, after she had only had it running a couple of hours after having nothing since midnight due to anesthesia for radiation, and not being able to have anything two hours before and after chemo. Don't tell the nurses, but this morning I gave her some honey vanilla Greek yogurt, in addition to the ice chips she is allowed to have. The speech therapist had said she would try soft food next session earlier in the week, but she can't do that during the times she can't eat, which is most of the day. She was able to swallow just fine.

Elise can speak well, but she won't do it very often. I asked if she is uncomfortable speaking, and she said yes, it is a little hard to breathe. Last night was rough in other ways as well. When they finally got her food going about 11pm, the pump was temperamental and kept beeping. Her heart rate monitor kept beeping every time it went past 120. The bed evidently had something blocking the electric eye because it kept lifting up automatically when the nurse, Angel, was trying to lower it. I didn't know the bed could get so high it could almost reach the heavens. It figures that would happen with a nurse named Angel. She is a fairly new nurse, and didn't know about the electric eye. It would have been funny if I was not so tired. So that's my story for skipping writing in the journal, and I'm sticking to it.

Today Marty is going to do some guided imagery meditation with Elise. He bought a digital recorder to record himself also, so Elise can listen to them any time she wants to. I found some scripts on a cancer website that help the patient to visualize the different immune system cells destroying cancer cells. The images are war -like/ violent, but the meditation starts and ends peacefully. Marty has professional experience with guided meditation/hypnosis, and Elise does not get annoyed with him or his voice, so I'm staying out of that endeavor.

Elise's morphine was cut by 50% yesterday, and she is down to just 1mg/day of Decadron (steroids) for brain swelling. Today her Cymbalta is being increased, so hopefully that will help her mood. Yesterday, Elise stood up three times with the physical therapist, and he said she did 90% of the work to stand. She was not able to take a step, though, because she was unable to bear all her weight on one side. I think that was yesterday, but it seems like I wrote about that already. She tried to take a sideways step the day before.

I just had to get it off my chest, so I just told the nurse about the yogurt. She said she can't give her anything, but...she gave me a wink, wink, nudge, nudge kind of look. Pasta shouldn't be far behind. All you kind people who brought us food, I have your containers and tote bags, but I don't know which belong to who, so give me a description and it's yours. Thanks for the delicious and nutritious food, and the effort you took to make it gluten free for Marty (those who knew). Oh, I almost forgot the most important thing. Elise has gone two nights and two days with her trach capped, with no problems breathing. The lung doctor chastised me for not making sure it was uncapped the first night, but she had gone twelve hours with no problem, and she has alarms for blood oxygen and heartbeat, and I am a light sleeper, so I didn't say anything when the nurses misunderstood the order or forgot. I tried to blame it on the nurses, but he said I should have watched. I didn't admit leaving it on purpose, but when I reminded him she did well, he said it could have been a different outcome. Of course he is right, but he doesn't know what a light sleeper I am. I think he was also ticked off because he had written an order for two hours as tolerated during the day. Then the ENT doctor came by later and put the capped inner cannula on her, and when he saw how well she did, he ordered she could have it on all the time during the day but we would wait for an overnight trial the next night. I didn't tell the lung doctor not to feel bad because I had not heeded the other doctor's order either. I am making myself sound like a dishonest weasel, but I do have integrity on other issues.

June 24, 2012 by Joy Pentz. You guys are wonderful. I get so much from reading your messages. Knowing the brain makes new cells and can re-wire/repair itself is very encouraging. One of Elise's nurses, Mandy, brought in three gifts for her today. A little bear with butterfly wings, a heart shaped pillow made by Project Have a Heart and a handmade afghan. Then she said she was bringing in something else, but Elise could not keep it. It was a wheelchair with a high back. We took Elise for a walk outside and visited the nurses in ICU. They were amazed at her progress. Project Have a Heart was inspired by a grandfather who believed the heartfelt notes and shared prayers of friends and family alike helped to heal him just as much as the treatments did. Volunteers make heart shaped, tied fleece pillows and pray for cancer patients of St. Vincent Cancer Care.

This morning Elise got her trach out. They put a dressing over her opening, and she has to press down on it if she wants to speak, which she does not. She says she will speak when it heals, which should be a few days to a week. She still has to have a swallow test before she is supposed to eat. I told the speech therapist about the yogurt, and she said that was risky because she may not have the ability to sense food or drink going down the wrong way, and that the reason they use ice chips and water is if they go down the wrong way the lungs can handle it. Other substances puts her at risk for pneumonia. So much for mother's intuition on that issue.

It was wonderful to speak with Emily and Matthew today. Emily has gotten pretty skilled at having a one way conversation with Elise, who nods and mouths words to her. Emily packed her suitcase for the birthing room. Four weeks till the due date. She wanted to know the details of labor, getting to the hospital and delivering my children. It's always a pleasure to relive those experiences. In England, all the ante-natal visits are with midwives. Every time I hear the word ante-natal, it makes me feel they are against babies, (pro and anti). The baby will be delivered by a midwife. The birthing room is attached to a hospital in case one is needed. Emily qualifies for the birthing room because she is low risk. She said there is a birthing pool, but four birthing rooms so you don't know if you will be able to use it. The birthing room has exercise balls and mats so you can stay active during labor. There is no bed. You heard me right, no bed. Hopefully, they put something sterile down to catch the baby while she is doing her gymnastics. Being with EEOC, I had to ask if any of the midwives were male, and if so, are they called midhusbands? Emily did not know of any midhusbands.

From: Pentz, Marty. Sent: Sunday, June 24, 2012 11:12 AM   I just realized that her trach is out. Such great progress. May 14th when they put her on the ventilator, and I thought she was going to die that day. Amazing that she is breathing on her own. God is good and prayer is wonderful. We keep shrinking tumor.

June 25, 2012 by Joy Pentz: For some odd reason I feel exhausted today, so I am going to update you by copying Marty's entry on Facebook. He has written some very moving entries over the course of this "adventure." 1241 hours Monday. It is hard to explain the feeling when your daughter is looking at you and you know she is actually seeing you. This is certainly what I would call a spiritual experience, but that does not seem to capture the whole essence of what went through me.

Today, when I called Joy, she gave Elise the phone and Elise said, "Hi Dad."
First time she has spoken to me on the phone since prior to May 12th.
Amazing. She had the trach removed yesterday and she took a couple of
steps on her own today and was able to stand on her own a couple of times
for about 3 minutes. Living with these changes daily brings such a smile to
my face that will not quit. Next up is eating and more talking. She liked the
guided imagery recording I made for her so I am scripting out another one
or two on self-worth, depression or learned happiness and loving your
mind.

We took her outside yesterday and having her outside of the hospital room
without a whole medical team and tubes was great as well. As many of you
know I read a lot. Lately everything that I have been attracted to reading,
novel or otherwise, has been about the power of love to transform
anything. Thank all of you for the love, prayers and blessings you have
bestowed on Elise and all of my family. The journey is long when I look
ahead, but with all of you I can more easily see only today and experience
Elise each day and the love all around us.

Sent: Monday, June 25, 2012 1:07 PM.   Too tired last night to get on the
computer. Elise is sleeping right now and Joy is talking to Emily about her
experience giving birth. Elise is continuing to improve. She has a cold right
now so that adds to the struggle. Feel blessed today to have the love in my
life I have. Walked in Harrison state park for about 45 minutes this morning;
much peace there. God is everywhere. Starting a new guided imagery for
Elise and so more later.

June 26, 2012 by Joy Pentz

The miracles keep coming. Today Elise had a swallow test, and she is now
authorized to eat. No more late night surreptitious yogurt. It was very
interesting to watch the test at Elise's bedside. They brought in a monitor
and a probe with a camera to insert through her nose into her throat. I
could see the vocal cords and opening to the trachea. The ice chips, water
and applesauce were green so they could be seen on the monitor. She was
also given cheese and then cheese with crackers. When she swallowed, the
epiglottis flapped over the trachea to protect the airway. She did beautifully
according to the speech therapist. She can now order food that can be

chopped up. In a couple of days she will be able to eat what she wants, and the nasal/gastric feeding tube will be removed.

The other good news is Hook Rehab looked at her chart and it looks like she can be admitted Saturday after she is done with radiation. She will have to do an hour each of speech, physical and occupational therapy each day. I hope they don't ask her if she wants to do it like they do here. She gets tired out very easily, and is apt to say no. She declined to stand during physical therapy today, but she did reaches while sitting to strengthen her core and balance. Marty's entry about Elise standing and walking by herself was a bit of a miscommunication. Still miraculous, but not quite as advanced yet. She was able to stand by herself for a few seconds after the therapist helped her get to a sitting position and then to a standing position. She was able to take a step, but only if the therapist stands so that she puts her leg against Elise's knee to keep it from buckling while Elise moves the other leg. She told the therapist she is scared she will fall trying to walk. The therapist told her she has not dropped a patient in all of her 30 years on the job.

Understandably, Elise has lots of fears right now. Elise is reluctant to talk right now, but assures us she will talk once her neck is healed from the trach. She said a few things today, and left a voice message for Marty. Marty got the message, but could not hear it. I am still so tired, but Marty has not posted on Facebook today, so I can't take a short cut like I did yesterday. Thanks so much for all your love, support and prayers.

From: Pentz, Marty: Sent Tuesday, June 26, 2012 9:16 PM Our miracle girl just keeps amazing everybody, including the Drs. Today after she successfully passed her swallow test she ate mac and cheese and sherbet, mostly sherbet. Elise has two more chemo treatments and three more radiations. After this phase of treatment she will get chemo five days per month. After the MRI in about 4 weeks, that I believe will show little or no cancer left standing, we will decide upon next steps. She will probably be going to inpatient rehab at Hook rehab at community east hospital this coming Saturday. Those of you who saw her anytime in the past two months know how amazing her progress has been. She spent a week there prior to going to Houston for treatment. She will be getting at least three hours of therapy daily at that time. Once she is in inpatient rehab Joy can come home. We can only be there during visiting hours or when we are asked to be there for therapy. I imagine it being hard not being able to go there whenever I want to. Joy has been living with her since May 12th. Watching her eat by herself and wanting to eat is mythic progress.

I had to have part of my big toenail removed today because it was in-grown. In many of these posts I have been attempting to describe the in-describable with this experience. Words like miracle, magic, blessing, love, courage to keep fighting by Elise, perseverance. None of them quite do this justice. Buddhism and Christianity both talk about transcendence. This seems to fit what I have been trying to say. In Buddhism transcendence is often described as climbing or going beyond. Other religions may see transcendence as God both within and beyond the universe. God has been within this entire journey with Elise, Joy and everybody else. This has been a transcendent experience for me. I don't know if I thank all of you enough for your prayers and other forms of help. Please accept my heartfelt and soul felt thanks. Marty

June 27, 2012 by Joy Pentz: Elise surprised herself by not having that much of an appetite and getting full with a few bites. She had oatmeal with banana, and ate it all, but for lunch and dinner, just a few bites of pasta and orange sherbet. The doctors are going to leave in her feeding tube until she is eating enough food. For physical therapy she walked with lots of assistance holding on to a walker which one of the therapists moved for her. She walked about 4 steps forward and 4 steps backward. Elise looks more lively and stronger every day. Her depression is improving to about a 4, and she is sleeping less. Last day of chemo tomorrow, and last two days of radiation forever.

Sent: Thursday, June 28, 2012 8:14 AM from Marty Pentz. At work, but do not start for another 15 minutes. This writing has been very good together, along with Joy's in some type of format for Elise. She continues to progress in her ability to eat and is talking a little bit more. She is ready to move to the next step. Her greatest expressed fear is still that she will be "stupid." Anything anybody can do to help her with this would be greatly appreciated. Joy has been quite tired the last few days and it is really good that she will be forced to be home this weekend as Elise can only have visitors at the inpatient rehab during visiting hours. The plan is still for Elise to go to the rehab hospital this Saturday. What a relief. I feel emotionally spent today. I have been eating poorly, but have started back on track today. There have been many blessings during this journey with Elise, closer with her and Joy, watching the wheels of the Fellowships we belong to lovingly turn, the kindness and compassion shared by those Joy and I work with and the continuing evolution of my spiritual life. Gratefully the journey continues. Our whole family loves music so this quote seemed appropriate for today: "Music is well said to be the speech of angels." Thomas Carlyle

June 29, 2012 by Joy Pentz. I missed updating last night because I fell asleep. I guess the adrenalin is running out. We just found out Elise is going to rehab this evening. She will be going to Hook Rehab, which is inside Community East Hospital. A little over a month ago, we were not sure if she would leave here. Now she is better than she has been in months, and improving. Thanks be to God and the host of prayers you have sent up on her behalf.

June 29, 2012 by Joy Pentz: Here's tonight's post early because as soon as I get home and unpack and shower, I am going to sleep in my own bed! Today has been hectic, but good. Just as the physical therapist came to work with Elise, transport came to take her down for her LAST radiation. She was able to walk with the walker and two people beside her to get to the transport cart. The therapist had her left knee covered in case it buckled, but it didn't. Elise initiated all the steps herself. The technician who has been giving Elise her radiation gave her a Teddy bear for finishing. Everyone here has been so nice. I thought I was going to be able to have one more slumber party with Elise, but once the insurance approved Hook, we had to go. Elise told me she was annoyed and embarrassed at the questions I asked Dr. Jessica today. I know (and she told her friend) she will be glad to be alone in her room in Rehab. She did tell me she was glad I was with her at St. Vincent, though.

Elise will have a MRI on July 27 to see the results of treatment so far. They wait that long to be sure any swelling from the radiation and steroids is gone, and to let the radiation continue to do its job. Then she will have chemo with pills (Temodar) the first five days of each month, and chemo with a drip called Avastin on day one and day 15. That will continue for a year if the tumor remains stable or shrinks or (hopefully) disappears. If the tumor starts growing, which it won't, we will have to find a clinical trial. It is my understanding that Avastin helps kill and prevent the formation of blood vessels the tumor forms to get nutrition.

All of Elise's lines have been removed except for the nasal/gastric tube. They will remove that as soon as she eats enough during the day. She is eating a bit more, but still needs to be supplemented by tube feeding at night to get the rest of the calories she needs. She gets Mighty Shakes (similar to

Ensure) with her meals, but it's still not enough. This is my last post from St. V. What an amazing six weeks this has been. Miraculous.

From: Pentz, Marty: Sent Friday, June 29, 2012 7:52 AM. Last day of radiation ever is today. Elise will be going to rehab hospital later today or tomorrow, most likely tomorrow. Anybody who saw her in ICU or the month or so prior to when she admitted to St. Vincent's on 12 May would be astonished at how well she is doing. The last few months before she went down real fast, her short-term memory was all but gone. Now she remembers who visited her a few days ago, what she ate for breakfast and so on. What a blessing. My memory is something I have not ever thought much about. Until this brain tumor/cancer I did not realize what a blessing a memory of any kind is. Memory is being added to my gratitude list. Before this recovery when she would eat she would not remember to finish chewing and swallowing before taking another bite. Yesterday she put her spoon down between each bite and waited until she swallowed to start again. I only reminded a couple of times to take her time. I took simple eating for granted as well. She is talking a little more each day. "While we try to teach our children all about life, our children teach us what life is all about." Angela Schwindt

July 1, 2012 by Joy Pentz. I fell asleep writing a journal entry last night. I think Elise is going to rehab faster than she thinks. All three of us were depressed a bit yesterday. I'm not sure why. Maybe because of the separation for me and the fact that she was in so much better shape last time she was at Hook. It's weird that she is in the same room she was in last time at Hook as well as the ICU at St.V. She had all three therapies yesterday and is scheduled for all three today as well. I won't be able to give first hand updates very often anymore. I spoke with the speech therapist yesterday, and she told me she is smart. I asked Elise if she told her the same thing, and she did. That is a big fear for Elise, and she is going to have to work at that.

Marty is visiting Elise several times a day because he feels like we abandoned her. He went back last night, and was happy they put her to sleep on her side, and she was able to stay on her side without pillows to support her. She sat up without being supported or holding on to anything while they were preparing a wheelchair for her. She has not had enough food by mouth to get the ng tube out yet. Her appetite has still not returned, and her stomach has not expanded enough to eat much before she gets full. She's lost some weight, which puts her at a good weight for her, before she started eating so much pasta. She ordered mac and cheese and lasagna at St V, and didn't like them, and now she won't order pasta.

I am writing this with Swipe, a new way to enter text that is like magic. You just go to each letter on the touch screen, lifting your finger only between words so a space is made. If we can put a man on the moon and create Swipe, there will be a way for Elise to recover.

From: Pentz, Marty. Sent: Sunday, July 01, 2012 10:51 PM. Just got home after kissing Elise goodnight at the hospital. She was sound asleep. She is making great progress. She walked today a number of steps with a walker, completed speech exercises for about an hour, including brief singing. She is eating more each day so should have the feeding tube removed tomorrow or Tuesday. Sometimes if I think too much this journey with Elise seems like such a long way to go, but one-day-at-a-time we will get to wherever we are going. I seem to be getting better at simply experiencing life and not looking very far ahead. I know her body needs a rest and time to physically recover, but I am finding it difficult to not think of her not having any active cancer treatment for a month. Another chance to practice just for today. Emily is due in a little over a month and I am so excited to be a grandfather. Cannot wait, now simply need to figure out when we can all go to England to see Emily, Matthew and the baby. "The best scientist is open to experience and begins with romance-the idea that anything is possible." Ray Bradbury. With what we are going through now I know that all illnesses are curable.

July 2, 2012 by Joy Pentz: Elise walked about 40 feet today with a walker. The therapist held on to the walker so it didn't roll ahead of her. Once in a while the therapist helped move her left foot. She was able to manipulate small items with her left hand. She is speaking much more often, and spent an hour in speech therapy. The people in rehab seem to really love Elise. She is still not eating enough to remove the feeding tube from her nose. Her nose is getting pretty red. Elise is not able to hold her head up for very long. The muscles on the left side of her neck are weak, so her head tilts to the right and causes neck pain. She is still depressed. It is hard for us to see her this way. Please keep praying and sending your hopeful messages.

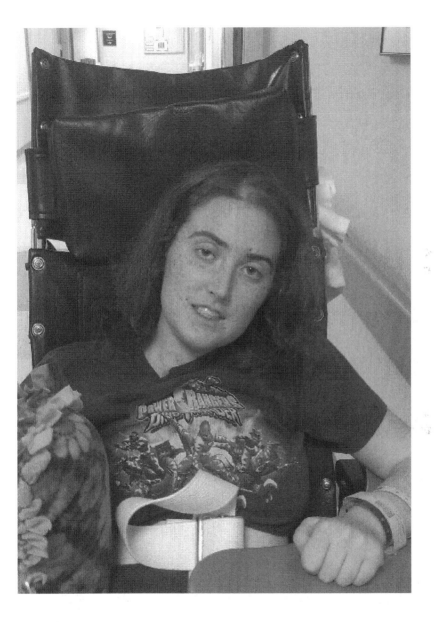

ELISE GOT HER FEEDING TUBE OUT. SHE DOES NOT HAVE THE STRENGTH TO
HOLD HER HEAD UP STRAIGHT, AND NEEDS THE SUPPORT OF A HIGH-BACK
WHEELCHAIR.

July 4, 2012 by Joy Pentz.   The good news is Elise's appetite is back. The bad news is she's been throwing up all day. Hopefully it's just from putting too much into a shrunken stomach. I am using talk to text to write this so any mistakes are not my fault. Last night after Elise ate everything on her tray she was able to get Andes mints out of the box and unwrap them. This morning Elise ate a huge breakfast and it was after that she got sick. She was not able to eat lunch or dinner. When we visited her today I got in bed with her and we listened to standup comedians. It was enjoyable until she threw up all over the bed. Marty was quite upset because nausea and vomiting can be a symptom of intracranial pressure but I think she would have had other signs such as headache and blurred vision. Drew visited with Elise earlier today and said she was in good spirits and even laughed at jokes he made. So I am going to remain hopeful that this is just a case of too much food.

> *Comment by Marty, January 18, 2018: On July 4, 2012, Elise could not hold her head up. Today she can drive. "The Age of Miracles is still with us."*

July 5, 2012 by Joy Pentz: YAY, no throwing up today! I can't believe I didn't notice first thing that Elise got her nose tube out. I knew something was different, but Marty noticed first. She ate well and enjoyed being visited by a handful of dogs. It was a much nicer visit today. Elise and I enjoyed reading your messages together today. Thanks so much for your prayers and messages.

From: Pentz, Marty Sent: Thursday, July 05, 2012 10:38 PM.   What an amazing roller coaster ride this has been. Elise had nausea and vomiting yesterday and today no nausea and able to eat. Biggest news today is she no longer has the tube in her nose. All artificial ports of entry are now gone. There was a time when she was in ICU that she had 5 different IV pumps at one time plus oxygen and the ventilator to keep her alive. Elise could not breathe and was in an apparent coma. Today she can walk short distances with a walker, and has some use of fine motor skills. All is slowly but surely coming back. What gets to me the most right now is the apparent lack of emotions, but she did physically move herself to a sitting position to pet the many therapy dogs that came tonight. She is moving forward fast. In retrospect the first symptom that was produced by this tumor was her diminishing of emotions. It looks like all the symptoms are going away in the order they appeared. God is good. Thank you all for being such a big part of this amazing journey.

July 7, 2012 by Elise Pentz: Hey this is Elise. I'm in Community East for rehab. Thanks for your prayers

July 8, 2012 by Joy Pentz.   I'm hoping I can talk Elise into writing another entry. We were enjoying reading your responses to her message when they came to take her away to the bathroom. She is on a 2 hour schedule and doing well with that. She really wants to walk and is working hard towards that goal. She has her telephone so you can call or text her. She called us at home today asking when she was going to get to eat Joe's pasta. That is the first phone call she has made in months so you can just imagine how good Joe's pasta is.

From: Pentz, Marty, Sunday, July 08, 2012 9:44 PM   Elise continues to improve at least a little each day. Today seemed like a quantum step ahead. She made her first phone call since about the 8th or 9th of May. She called home wondering where the pasta was that a co-workers of Joy's promised to bring today. She ate this for dinner. She stated the other day that she is most frustrated about not being able to walk on her own. She has been able to go about 40 feet with a walker and staff close at hand. With God's help and all the prayers and help from everybody it will not be long and Elise will be walking again. She was motionless for about 5 weeks so this recovery, while steady, will take a while. With Elise now having a cell phone she can take calls and text messages. She is not that good at answering yet, but it is good for her to hear from all of you. The gratitude I feel for her still being here and moving forward is beyond description. One of my favorite quotes by JFK is about gratitude and how I endeavor to live my life: "As we express our gratitude, we must never forget that the highest appreciation is not to utter words, but to live by them." John F. Kennedy

From: Pentz, Marty: Sent Monday, July 09, 2012 10:12 PM   Elise continues to progress physically and cognitively. She is still profoundly depressed. She may not be as afraid of her brain not working well, as she is improving quickly. In occupational therapy today she was able to correctly use analogies. She told her mom she is fearful she will not be able to walk and we try to keep her focused as much as possible on the progress she is making. She did say that she was glad she is getting better most of the time. Depression can be insidious, and with what she has been through most people would be depressed. When she smiled today it did look more like her old smile than it has been. I know the Spirit is with her and she will pass through this depression as well. Life can be so hard. I will keep praying and loving.

July 10, 2012 by Elise Pentz: I walked 150ft with a walker. Elise

July 11, 2012 by Elise Pentz: Hey, it's Elise. I just ate dinner. Thanks for the love and prayers

July 12, 2012 by Elise Pentz: I just ate dinner. It was good. I walked with only the help of one person today. Elise

"WICKED" IS ONE OF ELISE'S FAVORITE SHOWS. SHE IS WEARING THE TEE
SHIRT WHILE SINGING "AS LONG AS YOU'RE MINE." HER VOICE IS WEAK.
BOTH HER VOICE AND HER LAUGH ARE WEAKER THAN BEFORE THE
CANCER.

From: Pentz, Marty. Sent: Thursday, July 12, 2012 8:15 AM   Elise continues to improve in her physical abilities. She sang "As Long as You're Mine" from Wicked with her mother and the hymn "Morning has Broken" as well. If you ask her if she wants to sing she often says no, but if you put the music in front of her and start singing she will join right in. It did my heart and soul good to hear her sing after so long. Her depression remains profoundly deep. Talking with her social worker yesterday she will probably be at this rehab for 3-5 more weeks and then daily outpatient rehab. My faith is that she will come all the way back, but this depression scares me. She continues to work hard in therapy and sings, so she is pushing to find her way back in all aspects of life. You do not know how much it means to me to know that all of you are out there for us, praying and willing to do what is needed to be done. Thank you is not quite enough. Loving somebody is worth all the anguish. If I had not started on my journey of discovery over 30 years ago I would have missed all this love and peace. Even though the peace can be fleeting at times.

July 13, 2012. By Elise Pentz. Hey Todd this is your shout out. Hey Drew, today I had a wonderful breakfast of fruit and yogurt and cereal with a banana.

July 13, 2012 by Joy Pentz: I just wanted everyone to know that Elise is doing really well. Her mood is much improved and she is getting more and more independent. She is very motivated to walk by herself, and she is enjoying the different activities she does in therapy. It is so great that she is able to hold her head up straight and enjoys having conversations with us again. Thank you God!

From: Pentz, Marty: Sent Sunday, July 15, 2012 3:17 PM   Elise was without emotions for many months. Yesterday she fell when she tried to walk on her own. She started to cry and later said the tears were an amazing blessing from God. Her emotions are back. A number of her friends were there yesterday and she had them laughing and she was laughing as well. Elise is reading, talking and slowly beginning to walk again. I feel thoroughly blessed today. As I have learned over and over again in this life, there is great power in vulnerability. The fellowship I belong to asserts that to recover one has to "surrender to win." I have found that to be so accurate in my life, but never more so than this recent journey with Elise. The medical knowledge God has brought into this world has taken our family a long way and our faith has pushed us even further. My faith has also kept me at least partially sane over the past few months.

July 16, 2012 by Joy Pentz.   Enjoying my day off with Elise. She is getting feisty now, so I can't get her to do something easily. She's more like her old self, which is great, but I can no longer hand her my phone and get her to post to here. I'll try later. Today she walked 350 ft. with assistance. She asked if I was going to stay until dinner. She said she wants me to stay because she likes me. What a nice change. I really enjoy going to therapy with her. It's great to see the staff's excitement about her improvement.

> *Comment by Joy, January 12, 2018: It was fascinating to watch Elise do a test in Speech Therapy. They gave her a placemat size piece of paper covered with all the letters in the alphabet in no particular order. She was supposed to circle all the letter "R's." She quickly found all of them on the right hand side of the paper, but none on the left hand side of the paper. This was from "left inattention" caused by the brain injury on the right side. She had no vision problems. She just did not notice the entire left hand side of the paper. When she got out of the hospital, we had her name all the objects on the left side of the road wherever we drove to practice paying attention to the left.*

> *Comment by Marty, January 21, 2018: There is a bathroom off of our kitchen, and when Elise first came home from rehab, she would leave the bathroom and always turn right. She would go around the long way through the hallway, entry, living room and dining room. The kitchen is a few steps to the left of the bathroom. As fascinating as this was, it was much less so being my daughter.*

From: Pentz, Marty. Sent: Monday, July 16, 2012 9:44 PM. While watching a show with Elise, she laughed. Others had told me that she has recently laughed, but this was my first encounter with her laughing in at least 5-6 months. It was a joyous experience to hear her laugh. The journey ahead appears long, but it is a possible journey and we are traveling it today. This book I am reading called "The Challenge of the Soul: A Guide for the Spiritual Warrior" written by Rabbi Goldstein makes the point that the key to Karate as an art of war is spirituality and humility. I feel that in this war I have been fighting with Elise and her cancer my chief weapons have been spirituality, humility and surrender. Surrender to God for the results and ask for the result I want, spirituality to keep praying, asking others to pray, and meditate. What humility I can possibly see, is in asking God and others to help and knowing my limits when I need to talk to others or ask for help for yard work and such. I sometimes think too much and too deeply. I miss Elise being upstairs and going to meetings. Love is deep.

July 17, 2012 by Elise Pentz: Thanks for your posts. The food has gotten better. I can't wait to get out of here. I feel like I have just woken up. I kept falling asleep during therapy. Thank God for Provigil. My depression is down to a three. Elise (Dictated to Mom)

Sent: Tuesday, July 17, 2012 7:09 PM   Short, but wonderful tonight. Elise said, "I feel like I am alive and have just woken up." She even laughed at one of my corny jokes. What a blessing to hear her laughing and joking. Besides being a God of Love, I believe God is also a God who likes laughter. The journey continues.

July 18, 2012 by Elise Pentz: Hey everyone. It's Elise. Just ate dinner with my mommy. It was delightful. I did math problems and walked yesterday

From: Pentz, Marty: Sent Friday, July 20, 2012 10:14 PM   Elise continues to improve. She walked up 7 or 8 stairs today and baked cookies. She is laughing more and telling jokes as well. Much of her is back, and she can get herself into bed. I realized yesterday that while I feel great physically I am emotionally tired. Going to Evensong on Wednesday was great for me. Evensong in the Episcopal tradition is a service where everything is sung. Music is one of my balms as well as prayer and meditation. The spiritual life is to be lived every day, and I do what I can to accomplish this task. We keep loving daily.

From: Pentz, Marty: Sent Saturday, July 21, 2012 9:48 PM   Emily is due today, but apparently no baby yet. I cannot wait to be a grandpa. Hope to be able to go over to England soon. Joy and I had a long talk with Elise today at her behest. She wanted to know if we saw the old Elise back yet. Shared with her that her recent experiences can make her better or bitter and it was up to her. She agreed. She has some anger about all she has been through and cried some today. Great to see all her emotions as she also laughed some. She is walking mostly on her own with balance support through a gait belt. I am so grateful that she was talking like a "normal" 20-year old and wondering about life. A number of her friends from her Fellowship were there for a meeting today and more are coming on Tuesday. This is so good for her and those that come. The Presence of God in my life is a most precious part of my life. As so many over the years have shared with me, and a big part of my understanding of Ignatian spirituality, the Awe in life is most present when I am seeking God in the experiences of every day. I am seeing God in all of you who love Elise and our family, and the joy I feel in my love for my work. I miss Emily a lot.

July 23, 2012, by Joy Pentz. It's been a while since I updated. Elise makes it to the toilet all the time now. She walks well with someone holding on to her gait belt just in case. She is eating well. Her thinking and memory seem normal. She is less depressed and sometimes smiles without prompting. She started writing in the journal Angel, a St Vincent nurse, gave her. She is making others laugh again. Her friends knew something was wrong when she stopped trying to do that. She will have an MRI Fri and we'll see the status of the tumor. Gone we hope. Elise is back on Facebook and she is listening to her iPod. Her choral music cheers her up the most. Hopefully she will write here again soon. Keep praying. Thanks!

July 23, 2012, by Elise Pentz. Hello, this is Elise. I just ate dinner. I can't wait to get out of here. I'm still getting better every day so that gives me hope.

From: Pentz, Marty: Sent Monday, July 23, 2012 9:38 PM   Still not a grandpa. Elise continues to improve daily. This is a big week. We meet Wednesday with her rehab treatment team to determine next steps and progress to date. Friday she has an MRI to see what is physically happening in her brain. They are walking her most places now and she does this well. Taking each day as it comes is an amazing thing to be able to do. The following quote says how I feel about the blessing of being able to love Elise here on this "side of eternity." "We should certainly count our blessings, but we should also make our blessings count." Neil A. Maxwell

From: Pentz, Marty. Sent: Wednesday, July 25, 2012 8:46 PM   Elise has been transferred into the behavioral program of the rehab. She will be in the same room, but will now have group sessions of various kinds along with her individual three sessions per day. She has gotten so much better than I believe they expected so she will be in the hospital about another four weeks. She will have a six hour pass this Saturday. I sometimes find it hard to believe how well she is doing. I feel so blessed by God. She went bowling on an outing today and Daniel spent about two hours with her as well. She has an MRI tomorrow. The last scan was I believe on the 15th of May when I had serious doubts that she would live. We meet with the oncologist next Tuesday to discuss the results of the MRI and she starts the next round of chemo that day as well. She will be having five consecutive days of the Temodar she had before and 90 minutes two times per month of Avastin, both for a year. I am awed by the journey we are on, and the love from all of you. Now I need a grandbaby. The following quote is how I feel about being a grandpa and ongoing life with Elise. "A new baby is like the beginning of all things--wonder, hope, a dream of possibilities." Eda J. Le Shan

July 28, 2012 by Joy Pentz.   What a day. Both my daughters have stopped growing masses of rapidly dividing cells. We learned today from Elise's MRI that her tumor has shrunk about 61%! Emily's "mass of rapidly dividing cells" was born today. Oops, it's past midnight, so it was yesterday, July 27. Lilia Jane was born at 9:56 am U.K. time. She was born on her Daddy's birthday and the first day of the London Olympics not far away. Can't wait to see my first grandchild. Congratulations Matthew and Emily!

It has been so wonderful having my sister Carol here. Right before picking her up at the airport, we had a family meeting with the rehab team and trained with the therapists on how to take care of Elise while she is out on a pass. Drew went this morning to learn also which made Elise want to cry she was so touched. She wears a gait belt, and we have to hold onto it just in case she loses her balance. They showed us how to transfer her from bed to a chair and back, toilet and car. They actually have a car in the basement of the hospital for that purpose. The only problem she ever has is a little catch with her left toes sometimes when walking. She can even button her clothes now.

LEFT TO RIGHT: AUNT CAROL, ELISE AND HER MOM

Elise was transferred from the brain injury program to the neurobehavioral program this week. She is in the same room. It is just a more advanced program. She will continue individual therapy, but will add groups and outings. On Wed she went bowling. She had community group today where they made goals and will hold each other accountable. They also planned and will prepare a meal together. Ed and Joani, I would be worried about her being so determined she would leave when no one is looking, but they thought of that. Her bed is alarmed, and you have to get someone with a badge to open the door to let you off the unit. I really appreciate all your messages and prayers. We are witnessing miracles, aren't we?

Marty's updates on Facebook are much more philosophical than mine, and they are inspiring to read. I am planning on copying and pasting them all here in case you want to read them as well. We are filled with gratitude. Thank you God.

From: Pentz, Marty: Sent Saturday, July 28, 2012 4:51 PM   Lilia Jane. Wonderful, I am now a grandpa. Cannot wait until we can go to England.

Life is so precious. I already love this little girl so much. Hard to believe I am a grandpa. God is so good. Smiles and hugs all around.

July 29, 2012 by Joy Pentz. Elise was so excited last night she could hardly stop talking. She had a great time on her first pass. I told her how wonderful it is to see her happy and she pointed out that I haven't even been asking her to rate her depression anymore. Naturally I asked her then and she said she is not depressed! She was talking about wanting to have a job and being independent. She even said she would like to be a bilingual EEOC investigator. I had crocheted a hat for her which she wore on her pass and she asked if I could make her more in different colors. She rarely wants to wear things I make so this is so exciting for me to have her commission projects. Also the fact that she cares enough about how she looks to want to cover her bald spots is great too. She hadn't realized she had bald spots in back, so I took a picture to show her. Funny, Marty said he didn't realize he had more than a receding hairline until he saw his bald spot in back in our wedding pictures.

I'll post a photo with the hat I made when it dries. I had to retrieve it from the trash and wash it. Elise said she took it off when she laid down and it fell in the trash when she tried to put it on the nightstand, and she forgot to ask the nurse to get it out. If she hadn't asked me to make more hats or if she had not worn it on her pass I would have thought, "Likely story!"

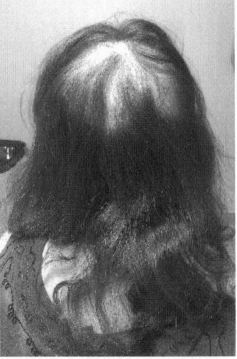

THE RAVAGES OF CANCER TREATMENT

"I DIDN'T MEAN TO THROW MY HAT IN THE TRASH"

From: Pentz, Marty: Sent Sunday, July 29, 2012 4:43 PM   Last few days have been an emotional rollercoaster. Emily gave birth to beautiful Lilia Jane on Friday and the results from Elise's MRI show that the tumor is 61% smaller than the scan taken on the 5th of May. I have been feeling the intense joy of Lilia's birth, Elise going out on a 6 hour pass and being with her friends and Drew's family and she appeared joyful and stated that she was. At the same time there is fear as the tumor is still there, and I was hoping and praying it would be gone. Thankfully I have not been alone since 31 October 1981 when I was two months without a drink and in despair I asked God for help (I actually said that something needed to change or I would be dead or drunk tomorrow). While I believe that God has always been with me, it was not until late in 1981 that I was willing to acknowledge God's presence in my life. Since that time I have learned to love and be loved by family and friends. Joy and I have been together on this journey since 1988 and are getting wonderfully stronger, closer and more in love with each other as we live life's joys and struggles together.

1435 hours, same day and back from a visit with Elise. She continues to improve daily. She starts the next round of chemo on Tuesday. Please continue to pray for the tumor to be gone, but also for her to handle the chemo with limited to no side effects and grace. Her boyfriend Drew has been full of love and Grace as well. He took Friday off to go to the hospital and be trained on how to help Elise in and out of cars and chairs so he could take her on her pass. I am experiencing love and seeing God everywhere. Today's quote: "Life is not measured by the number of breaths we take, but by the moments that take our breath away" by Anonymous

1632 hours the same day. Just spoke with Lilia Jane and Emily and Matthew on Skype. She is beautiful and they are all doing well. Took my breath away.

July 31, 2012 by Elise Pentz. Hello All, I'm just hanging out with my mommy. Daddy just left. We were singing old 60's songs together, and that was a hoot! I'm not glad I have cancer, but I'm glad I'm getting closer to my parents. I went for my first chemo drip today. It went smoothly. My daddy got me Panera Bread for lunch, which I ate during the infusion. It was great. Drew took me back to the hospital, and we got to spend some time together.

In PT, the therapist stretched out my ankle, and I used the foot peddler and arm bike to strengthen my limbs. In speech we watched some YouTube videos. I did some functional math (time and money story problems) in OT. My depression is ZERO! Thanks everybody. Elise

From: Pentz, Marty. Sent: Tuesday, July 31, 2012 8:56 PM   Excellent day today. Elise had appointment with oncologist and started second round of chemo today. Dr. was well pleased with her progress to date. On the way to the appointment Elise and I sang along to a CD by the choir she and I are in. They were Christmas carols and some other sacred music. The CD is called from Advent to Trinity. When I walked into her hospital room this evening she was listening to the Bridge over Troubled Waters CD by Simon and Garfunkel. We sang most of that and then some Beatles songs. It was great. As with many things in life there has been an immense amount of joy along with sadness, fear and anger throughout this cancer journey. Today was a day of joy. "I feel like a tiny bird with a big song." Jerry Van Amerongen.

August 1, 2012 by Joy Pentz: Elise's sense of humor is returning. Yesterday when the surgeon Dr. Y told her that her ventricles look good she said, so I have a good set of ventricles huh? Then when she was in the infusion room doctor Jessica asked how she liked the jungle theme. She looked at the large stuffed animals and jungle wallpaper and said like I don't have enough issues with fear having cancer. Neither of these doctors had seen Elise prior to for having a flat affect, so they were quite taken with her personality. It is wonderful to see the old Elise coming back.

From: Pentz, Marty. Sent: Thursday, August 02, 2012 9:11 PM   Elise is progressing so fast they told us today that they think she will be ready for discharge home on 17 August rather than the 24th. Another marvel among all we have had lately. Elise is coming home soon and I am a grandpa. The blessings keep coming.

From: Pentz, Marty. Sent: Tuesday, August 07, 2012 9:15 Elise has been struggling a bit of late. The chemo has caused some nausea and vomiting and increased fatigue issues. As one might expect nausea and fatigue also negatively impact her mood. She was some better today. We are working with Elise and her medical team to aggressively address these issues. She has, for now, agreed to modify how much and what she eats and they have increased her anti-nausea meds as well. Will work with the doctor tomorrow to see about the fatigue and maybe an increase in Provigil or an additional med. So much of her mood is tied to her ability to function. At age 20 I probably would have been no different. We all had a treat tonight. Members of the youth group from Lawrence United Methodist Church, where we attended for many years when the kids were young, came to the hospital to sing for Elise. They are led by three sisters that are amazing singers and call themselves the "Infinity Three" (aka The Bolton Sisters by others). They have a CD out that they give away and I will have soon. They sang Gospel songs as well as their own version of "Pray" by Justin Bieber and a song by Taylor Swift. Elise said it helped her mood "some," but it did wonders for mine. I have been praying, meditating, writing and talking with many people each day simply to survive all of this stress and often fear. God and the Fellowship I belong to give me much strength. Elise is still scheduled to come home on the 17th of August. She went into the hospital this time on the 12th of May. What a grueling and at times blessed journey this has been. "Without music life would be a mistake." Friedrich Wilhelm Nietzsche

August 8, 2012   by Joy Pentz. Elise is having nausea and fatigue. Her chemo round finished Sat, and she has not felt well since then. Her mood has also plummeted. She is getting more meds to try to control the nausea and she is eating less and avoiding dairy. Last night we were wowed by the singing of the youth corps from Lawrence United Methodist church who came to see Elise because one of the mothers has been so inspired by Elise's story thru Marty's fb posts. She is the mom of Infinity 3, the Bolton sister trio who are part of the youth group. They are extremely talented and delightful. They arrange their own harmonies, and I can't wait to get their CD. I will be going to England soon to help with my granddaughter, Lilia. It will be hard to be so far from Elise, but so grateful she is doing well enough for me to go. Skype is great, but grandma needs to hold her grandbaby.

From: Pentz, Marty. Sent: Wednesday, August 08, 2012 10:05 PM.   This is a rather long post as I had a lot I needed to say. 2136 hours the 8th of August 2012. Up and down day today. Work was more difficult than usual and Elise is still struggling with fatigue and nausea. By the time we left her at the hospital we were all laughing at some of the comments on caring bridge. It was so good to laugh. We appear to have a route ahead on treating the nausea and alleviating the fatigue.

At a meeting of the Fellowship I belong to tonight we discussed Spiritual Experiences and Spiritual Awakening. I was reminded that I need a deeper surrender than in the past. Or maybe it is simply surrendering more of life to God. Accepting Elise's cancer seems to mean to me that I am to do what I can to help eradicate this disease and love Elise as best as I can. Acceptance does not mean I like this road we are on, but that I will lovingly take this road with Elise, Joy, Emily, Daniel and all our loving family and when I surrender, even in part, for any given day, I have some measure of peace. One thing I sometimes forget is that I believe in my soul that Elise is in the warm embrace of God and always will be, here and on the other "side of eternity." With God I will be with her everywhere.

At times my ability to be patient with others has been in short supply. Elise is scheduled to complete this phase of her healing journey on the 17th of August when she will be discharged form Hook Rehab as ready for outpatient rehab. On the 23rd of August Joy is flying to England to be with Lilia, Emily and Mathew to see, bond and love our grandbaby. And of course our daughter Emily and her husband Matthew. At this point we cannot all go. While Joy is gone I will probably be enlisting the aid of many of you for various tasks, some that are already getting away from me. "In a world filled with causes for worry and anxiety ... we need the peace of God standing guard over our hearts and minds." Jerry W. McCant "Peace is not the absence of conflict, but the presence of God no matter what the conflict." Anonymous

August 9, 2012 by Joy Pentz: When we visited Elise last night she was very tired. She had been taking medicine for nausea all day. She also had difficulty walking due to her foot drop on the left side. We left a message for the physical therapist about using her boot again. She slept through her outing to the Scottish Rite Cathedral. By the time we left after dinner she was more alert. We had some good laughs; laughter really is the best medicine."

Pentz, Marty. 08/11/12 6:14 PM >>> Life can be so bleeping difficult at times. Prior to starting chemo and Avastin the first of this month, Elise was getting to be more like her old self again. The last few days, she has been more and more confused with short-term memory problems. Confusion is a common side effect of both these drugs, hence the term chemo brain. On the bright side she is going on a pass tonight to get her 18 month token and have some dinner with friends. She will also be home next Friday the 17th. We see the oncologist on Tuesday so we will discuss this confusion and what to do about it. We got a letter the other day from our homeowners association asking us to cut down a dead tree in our front yard. May get to this in the spring. It is not quite dead yet and there are two others they

cannot see that are also dead. Tempted to call them and tell them to go f...
themselves. Without God, loving family and friends, and a powerful
Fellowship I do not know how people survive things like cancer in a child.
Just stopped to cook some bacon and found it rather peace inducing, maybe
I need to cook bacon daily. Listening to a Mozart piano concerto also helps.
Skyped with Lilia, Emily and Matthew today. Lilia was awake, this was so
cool. Joy will be over there soon and that will be good. We are going to
Skype from the hospital tomorrow so Elise can see all of them. This writing
feels rather disjointed and stream of consciousness so will stop before this
gets much longer. "Faith is taking the first step even when you don't see the
whole staircase." Martin Luther King, Jr. On surrender and letting go and
letting God "If you believe that feeling bad or worrying long enough will
change a past or future event, then you are residing on another planet with
a different reality system." William James

August 12, 2012 by Joy Pentz: Elise gets to come home Friday. She is
extremely fatigued, but her nausea is under better control. Her friend Deb
brought her some ginger, and that helps along with avoiding dairy, eating
small meals and staying hydrated. Her depression is back and she
sometimes says she doesn't want to live. All these things started as she was
finishing her round of chemo. We visited with Emily, Matthew and Lilia on
Skype today. Elise was excited to meet her new niece, and looking forward
to holding her in Dec hopefully. Matthew said since she likes pet therapy so
much, she will love baby therapy. I suggested she could volunteer at a
hospital nursery to rock babies. Elise was supposed to go into a full day
rehab program as an outpatient, but that is uncertain now because of low
stamina. Keeping her off nausea meds is helping because they cause
drowsiness, but she is still very tired. It is so hard to see her get worse so
quickly and dramatically. One good sign through, she is finding me annoying
again.

August 14, 2012 by Joy Pentz: Your messages are so precious to us. Thank
you. Elise seemed so much better yesterday. She has not had meds for
nausea in a few days. She was able to do all her therapies yesterday. She is a
bit confused and having short term memory problems but these are side
effects of chemo. They came on so suddenly along with the other side
effects so we don't think they are caused by tumor growth. It's scary for us
because this happened when her tumor grew before. She gets her twice
monthly Avastin drip today. We hope this does not set her back. The other
chemo drug Temodar she takes by pill on days 1 thru 5 each month so she

has a couple of weeks before she takes it again. She will continue this schedule for a year as long as the tumor remains the same or shrinks. If it grows we have to find a clinical trial.

August 16, 2012 by Joy Pentz.   Tomorrow is the big day Elise gets out of the hospital. She will be home for the first time in about three months. We are all very excited. She did not seem to be too bothered by the Avastin drip she had Tues, so maybe it's the Temodar pills she takes the 1st five days of each month that hit her so hard. That's better because she has the Avastin twice a month. She is not having nausea, and is less tired. She is a bit confused and depressed, but hopefully that will get better also. I started a support planner on caring bridge which you can link to from the Welcome/My Story page. So many of you have asked how you can help, and you have all helped by your visits, support, prayers, messages and cards, but for those who have the time and want to do more, we will post specific items on planner, and you can sign up. Thanks everyone!

August 21, 2012 by Marty Pentz: Elise finished her evaluations at outpatient rehab today. Gratefully she will be in what they call the track program. Tuesday through Friday from 0845-1645. She appears to be getting a little better every day. Still some memory issues, but her balance is much better and walking as well. She can do all her own self-care with support, but cannot be left alone yet. Three weeks ago Elise could not cut up her own meat. Sunday while at dinner at Drew's parent's house, I sat in wonder and watched her cut up her own steak. I am learning to take nothing for granted. Feel blessed that Joy can leave Thursday to see Lilia, Emily and Matthew in England. I cannot wait to see them at Christmas. I have a lot of what I need as far as care for Elise is concerned. Still working on the rest of what I need, but with all the offers this will get done as well. I feel blessed to have a journey to take with Elise. "Reflect on your present blessings of which every man has many, not on your past misfortunes, of which all men have some." Charles Dickens

August 23, 2012 by Joy Pentz: Your messages are so inspiring. Thank you. On my way to the airport. Marty is so wonderful to encourage me to go. You are in for a real treat to read his entries while I'm gone. So inspiring. Elise is struggling about smoking. It and food are comforting to her. She is at a higher risk of a blood clot that can kill her while on Avastin. She said she'll just quit taking it instead of quitting smoking. Pray for her willingness to quit. That's what she's doing too.

Marty's thoughts, August 23, 2012 2034 hours. I was not going to write tonight because I have been in kind of a pissy mood, but decided I needed to write. I find it quite ironic the better Elise is doing the more my emotions appear to be on the surface. There was a mix-up in the time of her family conference on Tuesday, was not a big deal, but I started crying. Having all my emotions so close to the surface is an interesting experience I do not believe I want all the time. It is awesome to watch her slowly get back into life by being with her friends and having energy to go all day. Then five minutes later fear of her mental confusion when she woke up from a 2.5 hour nap and took her meds for the next morning that she just took 5 hours earlier. Thankfully the more potent meds are all taken at night. Thankfully, I think we have the solution to that snafu not happening again. Then I laugh out loud watching the Big Bang Theory. Joy is on her way to England and I miss her already. I know she will have a joyous time with Emily, Lilia and Matthew. Nothing I have been able to do lately would have been remotely possible without God and the Fellowship I belong to carrying me to my 31 years of continuous clean and sober time when I wake up tomorrow morning. That fateful call to my brother Steve on the 23rd of August 1981 was the butterfly that started many blessings and storms on their way. And now Elise is on this journey as well. "The strongest have their moments of fatigue." Friedrich Nietzsche.   Besides the genius from a previous quote I am much fatigued. Often it is emotional and physical fatigue. Getting some yard work done will help this as well as golf on Saturday.

August 25, 2012 by Marty Pentz: 2051 hours... Spoke with Joy and Emily on Skype today. It was wonderful seeing Joy holding Lilia. I am looking forward to seeing them at Christmas. Elise continues to improve and that is such a blessing. She starts her next five days of chemo on Tuesday. It was tough on her the last round. I am blessed to have some friends coming over in the morning to help with some yard work and electrical work I need done. My sister Kaye is coming over tomorrow afternoon to help me decide what to put on the caring bridge site for what help I need and when. I played golf today for the first time this year. I had a good time. I feel Blessed by God. Today was not as much of a struggle as it has been at time. I made Tilapia, kale and baked potatoes for dinner tonight, and it was good. It is time for bed so that is all for today. "I never think of the future, it comes soon enough" Albert Einstein

August 26, 2012: Hi all! This is Kaye Pentz, Marty's sister. I will be coordinating the Support Planner for Marty and letting him know who is coming with what. We created two recurring tasks today. I will be learning how to use the planner through the next few days so please bear with me. There is a way to invite friends and family to the planner but I don't have a "guest list" so will just send out this general invite on the Journal. You can sign up for it by clicking on Support Planner at the top of this page. Mainly it will be meals every other day delivered to Marty's home and mowing weekly. If something else comes up I will put out the word. I visited with Marty, Elise and Drew today. Elise is continuing to improve, which is wonderful!! Marty was in a pretty good mood today. He is having dinner with Drew's parents along with Elise and Drew and mentioned he will not be posting on Facebook and Caring Bridge tonight. Elise's transportation to outpatient rehab on Tuesday-Friday will be covered by Drew's sister. It is closer to home than inpatient rehab was, so that is good for all involved. Thanks for all your support and prayers. You and God are the reason they are hanging in there. Kaye

August 27, 2012 by Marty Pentz, 2156 hours. Watching baseball and having a little peace at this moment. Elise had a good day today. She went to Target with Drew's sister and was able to walk through the store without aid. Was also able to see and talk with Joy, Emily and Lilia on Skype as well. My emotions continue to be up and down, but I have become ok with that. It is simply the way I am right now. Elise has Avastin and sees her oncologist in the morning and starts outpatient rehab at 1300 hours. She is moving forward. Without prayer, meditation, love from my family and everybody and Anglican hymns I listen to daily I am not sure how I would handle all of this. The Fellowship I belong to has been such a blessing for me all these years and especially now. My sister Kaye was over yesterday for a visit and to help set some things up. It was great to see her. Grace, one of our priests at Trinity, was by today to see Elise and it was good to talk with her about what I am doing spiritually. All in all today was OK. "Laugh as much as you breathe and love as long as you live." Author unknown.

August 28, 2012 by Marty Pentz. 2109 hours. Just heard from a Fridley High School friend, with whom I played football. We were both linebackers. Playing football was a lot of fun. I remember running down on kickoff coverage like an idiot and just loving it. This Facebook thing is growing on me.

Elise had the Avastin again today and started another five days of the chemo drug Temodar. She does not seem to have any side effects from the Avastin, but last month about the 4th day into her five days of Temodar she started having nausea and increased fatigue. These side effects lasted about 4-5 days. We are taking a number of steps to attempt to minimize the nausea and fatigue, but it is hard to not feel like I am waiting for another shoe to drop. It was wonderful to hear from Jim today.

Also spoke with Joy again by Skype and was able to see Lilia again. Skype is growing on me as well. I am in a spiritual book and life study with a small group of men. We have been meeting for many years. Tonight we finished a book called "What is Ignatian Spirituality?" One of the sections that struck me tonight was on consolation and desolation. Consolation was defined one way as "every increase in hope, faith and charity." And Desolation as "darkness of soul, disturbance..." I take Consolation to mean when I am actively working to stay connected to God and Desolation as those times when I move away from God. Talking with Jim tonight and finding out that Janet is going to bring us dinner on Thursday have both increased my consolation. I am blessed to have all of you in my life, especially Joy, Elise, Emily, Daniel, Matthew, Lilia and Drew. Even with all that is going on in my life that I see as patently unfair, I feel blessed tonight. Goodnight.

August 30, 2012 by Marty Pentz, 2050 hours   I was not going to write tonight, but lying in bed I found my mind racing and unable to sleep. Sometimes, especially at night, I can hardly believe there is a tumor in Elise's head. Journaling has always been helpful to me. This just happens to be very public journaling. Janet brought us a great dinner tonight. It was really nice to sit around the table and eat with Elise, Drew and Daniel. Thank you Janet, a friend of ours Joy met through folk dancing and book club. She made it possible to enjoy a great meal together without wearing myself out even further. I will have some time to chill this weekend as the holiday gives me a break. Joy's sister Carol is coming to visit Elise this weekend. Elise wants to see her and asked her to come. I am looking forward to seeing her as well. Deb and Mike, my yardwork angel this past Sunday, are coming Saturday to bring dinner. And oh yea, Deb will be massaging Elise's feet and hands as well. Elise is better. This is her third night of this chemo round and her nausea has been quite manageable. Back to rehab tomorrow. "As we come to know humility, we realize our own human emptiness before the God who desires to fill us with divine life." David L. Fleming.

September 1, 2012, by Marty Pentz, 2156 hours. This has been a good day. It is now the first of September and it does not seem so long until Joy comes home. I miss her so, but I am so grateful she is able to be in England with Emily, Lilia and Matthew. I had a good day with Elise today. She has been such a trooper with all the treatments and therapy. We went together to a meeting of the Fellowship I belong to and then breakfast. Elise spent most of the afternoon and evening with Joy's sister Carol who flew in today for a short visit.

I went to an Indiana Fever basketball game tonight with a friend of mine. Somehow even with cancer life goes on. Deb and Mike, friends of Elise's who are quickly becoming our friends, brought dinner tonight. Gluten free spaghetti and meatballs and it was great. Deb then massaged Elise's feet, hands and colon. Elise wanted me to be sure to state that the colon massage was from the outside.

My emotions since all this began December 10th of last year have been all over the map. There have been many times, especially in May when Elise was so sick, that we did not know what to do. I simply trudge along moment to moment and work to find some joy in each day. Driving home from work yesterday I got so angry at this tumor and the unfairness of it. Thankfully I do not go there very often and just love the people in my life today. Living life being willing to feel all my emotions is exceedingly difficult at times, but is the only way I know to be fully alive. I am so grateful that I believe and trust in God.

September 3, 2012 by Marty Pentz, 1614 hours, I went for a 22 minute walk with Elise today. She did well, but was tired at the end. For her to be able to walk at all is a blessing. Elise is napping right now. Joy's sister Carol is on her way home. She is taking Daniel to dinner and then to the airport. Her visit was good for Elise and gave Drew and me a little break as well. Daniel and I Skyped with Joy, Emily and Lilia this morning and then Elise and Carol were able to talk with all of them this afternoon. It does me so much good to be able to see them as well as talk with them. I feel so blessed to have all these beautiful females in my life. It all starts with Joy.

I feel at peace right this minute; this house is so quiet right now. I have been reading this little booklet my friend John gave me on the Christian mystic, Julian of Norwich. My bachelor's degree is in the scholastic study of world religions. One of my classes was entitled something like "Mystical Literature." One of the books we read was "Showing of Love" by Julian of Norwich. Whenever I read her writing it touches something inside of me. When I ask the question, Why Elise, I do not get an answer. When I pray and meditate and read people like Julian of Norwich I still do not get happy answers. In this little booklet she is quoted as saying, in response to the black plague and other tragedies in her life: "Why me? Because I'm alive, and suffering and loss are part of all life." She goes on to assert that part of God's promise is that we are bigger than our suffering. This reminds me of one of my friend Kent's favorite quotes form Viktor Frankl that goes something like this: "do not ask the meaning of life, but what is life asking of me." I often feel quite small these days and that life is asking too much of me. I am sustained by the love from family and friends and the belief that God is with Elise and all of us all the time.

September 5, 2012 by Marty Pentz, 2214 hours the 5th of September 2012. Parts of this day were good and parts were quite stressful. First of all I want to sleep and cannot yet. Elise went back to choir tonight as she wanted to sing. She left fairly soon as she cannot sing like in the past and wants to work on this some more. Thankfully she agreed to sing some with one of the professionally trained singers in the choir to work on her voice and help her with voice therapy. She is moving forward. I miss Joy so much and more every day. I am grateful she can spend so much time with Emily, Lilia and Matthew. Work has its own issues, but I will ignore them for now. Continuing last night's theme: Julian of Norwich is quoted as saying "In God's love our life is everlasting." The pamphlet goes on to say "How could Julian be so hopeful in the face of the Black Death, terrible famines . . . For the simple reason that she believed with all her heart that God is Love." I agree with her. Goodnight

September 7, 2012 by Marty Pentz,   2223 hours. Was watching the show stand up to cancer tonight and when Tim McGraw sang "Live like You Were Dying," I started to cry. Crying felt good. Elise has done well today and is out with Drew and some friends. The days are long, and often fruitful, but the nights are all too short. I did my best today and I felt like it was enough. I seem to be doing ok handling my difficult emotions, but my daily household chores are beginning to get beyond me. I plan to get some caught up this weekend with a little play time. Joy is loving her bonding time with Lilia, Emily and Matthew, but I still miss her more than I thought possible. Many of us are loved by a number of people, but we do not always experience in our hearts and souls this love. I am convinced that my experiences of God allow me to more fully experience the love that Joy and the kids have for me. I feel their love for me more powerfully than ever before and I attribute this to all of us being more open to God and what the universe has to offer.

Through this difficult time with Elise's cancer I have felt more love and given more love than ever. I have been told many times since I have been writing about this experience that people I know and don't know have cried over what I have written. I feel blessed that some of who I am that I write about moves people. Much of my writing seems to come flowing out of my heart and soul. I am getting quite tired so goodnight for now.

September 10, 2012 by Marty Pentz, 2005 hours. I have not written in a few days. Mostly I have been missing Joy. The choir Elise and I sing in was back to singing this past Sunday. I so love singing Anglican Sacred music. Elise is not quite ready to sing yet as she cannot yet sing very loud or reach notes she used to be able to reach. She sings with me in the car so she is still singing some. We had a great time Skyping with Joy, Emily, Lilia and Matthew today. Elise, Daniel and I on this end. Without faith I do not know how people deal with normal life, much less when life is difficult. As I have shared in the past I have had times in my life of despair and desolation when I surrendered as much as I may be able to and found my way back with God's help to peace. The last few days I have been up and down emotionally, but I have some serenity tonight. A lot of my up and down is I am simply tired. Elise has oncology appointment tomorrow and Avastin so I get to sleep to six or seven am   "Love beauty; it is the shadow of God on the universe." Gabriela Mistral quotes (Chilean poet, 1889-1957)

September 10, 2012 by Marty Pentz, 0042 hours the 11th of September 2012. I cannot sleep yet. Sometimes my mind will not shut down. I will sing quietly in my bedroom and sing a couple of Psalms and then will try and sleep again soon. I so love the people in my life, especially those closest to me and I am sometimes scared. The quiet of the late night can be soothing at times and at others too quiet. It is time for me to be with God in solitude. Goodnight.

September 12, 2012   Hey everyone! It's Elise this time. I'm in outpatient rehab at Hook these days. It's going pretty well. I made a creamy mushroom pasta today during occupational therapy. It was delish! And there are still leftovers too! My dad is listening to "For my Lady" by the Moody Blues, him and my mom's song. I think it makes him miss my mom even more. "As life goes drifting by, like a breeze, she'll gently sigh."-For my Lady. We've been Skyping with my mommy, Emily and Lilia a bit too. I really miss my mommy! I'm going to make her a pumpkin pie before she gets in. I get to see her Monday, and I'm excited! Thanks again for all your prayers and caring words, it really helps me feel supported in this time of trial.

September 12, 2012 by Marty Pentz, 2140 hours. When one is emotionally awake life can be such an adventure. With a good night's sleep last night I had quite a good day. I was better able to ignore the bureaucracy at work and simply enjoy my work. Elise wrote an update on Caring Bridge tonight and then we read a number of what some of you have written to her and us on that site. She loves reading what you all write. She is feeling some better just about every day. Singing at choir practice tonight was a great experience as it always is. Elise is not yet ready to sing in choir, which will come. I just love to sing and singing to God simply does something to my soul and heart. From this piece of music we sang tonight by Boyle and called "Thou, O God, Art Praised in Sion." The line that touched me the most was "Thou wilt keep him in perfect peace whose mind is stayed on Thee." And from an Antiphon by Vaughan Williams "Let all the world in every corner sing, My God and King." There is still joy in the world and my Joy comes home on the coming Monday. Goodnight and sleep with God.

September 13, 2012 by Marty Pentz, 2118 hours. Elise's physical therapist told me today that she does not need 24-hour observation anymore. She can physically do what she needs to do, can safely walk stairs and take care of her daily needs. She cannot yet drive or cook without supervision. This is the same Elise that in mid-May could not walk, was then unconscious for three weeks and took another three weeks simply to get out of bed. Between God, loads of Love and modern medicine she has been the recipient of many ongoing miracles. I feel so blessed. These were my thoughts earlier today. Stress can do funny things. It appears that with all the support and help I gladly receive from God, family and all the rest of you amazing people I can survive and sometimes even thrive under great stress.

But sometimes little things undo me. For many months now we have been working to have a healthy and healing diet. Not sure if I have written this here before, but shortly before Elise went into the hospital in May we were eating a lot of kale. I had purchased this a number of times in Kroger and could not find it. I started to cry and yelled out "where is the f...ing kale." They brought me kale quickly. Tonight after folding a number of loads of laundry I noticed a light out in the hall and started to cry. Amongst a very blessed day, some frustration and exhaustion. Singing this Psalm verse is helpful: "In the multitude of my thoughts within me thy comforts delight my soul." Goodnight. (Psalm 94:19)

September 16, 2012 by Marty Pentz, 2109 hours. Joy is coming home tomorrow. Hard to describe how good I feel writing that statement. This past 3.5 weeks has been a challenge and a joy. Challenging in asking for help and while I can do this today it does not always come easily. The joy has been in getting closer to Elise and Daniel and having all of you be so willing to help. Elise was singing in our house yesterday. It has been many months since I heard her singing songs of love for God. Elizabeth, a fellow choir member and one who sings like an angel, came to our house and sang with Elise. It was great to hear them together and Elizabeth's encouragement of Elise is getting her to sing. Singing has always been one of the things that opens Elise to the love of God. Elise is thinking of rejoining choir on the coming Wednesday rehearsal at whatever level she is able. I love singing. "A bird doesn't sing because it has an answer, it sings because it has a song." Maya Angelou

September 18, 2012by Marty Pentz, 1757 hours. Joy is home. She arrived safely last night. I missed her so much and now she is home. It is such a relief to have her home. Elise is also immensely grateful her mother is home. My sister-in-law Connie and my niece Angie are coming into town later this week. It will be great to see them again. Elise has another MRI this Friday and we will see how much the tumor has been shrinking since the last one. I have some fear around this, but will simply keep praying.

2026 hours: Had a short break from writing. Today has been a very good day. Joy is home, Elise is better and I am going on a silent retreat September 28-30. I have been doing these retreats about once per year for some time now and find them tremendously life affirming. The Priest will speak 5 or 6 times on the theme for the weekend and then we pray and meditate on our experience of God. I want to know the experience of God in all of my life. If I pay attention I can see God speaking to me in many facets of my life, but I have to pay attention. I do not believe for a minute that God caused Elise's cancer. I do see God's love in all the outpouring of love and support from all my family and friends. "All the things in this world are here so that we can know God more easily." David Fleming, SJ. I see God in Janet bringing us tasty and healthy dinners the last three Thursdays; I see God in Lisa providing a great chicken and rice dinner two Sundays ago; I see God in Mike helping me with yard work: I see God in Deb giving Elise massages to help her feet heal and give her love and comfort; I see God in Grace coming to see Elise and to pray with us at our home and in the hospital; I see God in the choir members that sang at the hospital when Elise was so ill and all looked pretty grim; I see God in Elisabeth singing with and helping Elise to sing and enjoy singing again; I see God in the immense Love that Elise and Joy have for each other; I see God in the peace and great love I saw on Joy's face when she was holding our grandbaby Lilia in England; I see God in the thousands that have been on Caring Bridge and all those I have not mentioned. I see God in all of you and acknowledge you for the love in your heart.

September 21, 2012 by Marty Pentz, 2017 hours. This is the completion of an amazing day. Elise had an MRI today and the tumor keeps shrinking and has receded from her brain stem. Her clinical symptoms are all getting better and better. Her oncologist described her recovery as "remarkable." We looked at the MRI from May, the tumor was huge, and today and I said "how did she live through that?" The doctor said something like "I do not know." We continue forward with God, prayer, love from all of you, Avastin every two weeks and Temodar (chemo) for five days every four weeks. Elise is also continuing with four days a week of rehab. This healing journey is joyous today. It was great to have Joy with us today to get this news; she is blessedly home from her great trip to England. I thought I would write a lot tonight, but I really have no more to say than what I have said and that God is good.

September 21, 2012 by Joy Pentz: Hi everyone. I'm back. Today's MRI was such a relief, especially the fact that the tumor has receded from Elise's brain stem. She is getting better every day. She is talking about taking an economics or Spanish class next semester. She is also interested in taking a drawing class. She has done amazing pencil drawings, and I suggested she could give her art work to people who agree to make a donation to brain cancer research. She likes that idea. Elise is smoking and eating more because it is a comfort to her. I suggested trying to use her creative talent for comfort as well as to keep her hands too busy to smoke. She said when she pictures herself drawing, she sees herself doing it with a cigarette in her mouth. Well, I tried. She is not ready to give it up, but she told her doctor she would try to cut back. She has been eating all the cancer healing fresh fruits and vegetables I give her, so she is often too full to eat unhealthy food. She has a strong will to live now, and her mood is much better. She feels more like her old self. We are so grateful. Thank you for all your support. Joy

September 23, 2012   by Marty Pentz: 2147 hours. Friday and Saturday were such emotional highs that I sort of crashed today. Getting the news that Elise's brain tumor continues to shrink and is out of her brainstem was quite the high. Joy is home and all of Elise's clinical indicators; physical from scans and physical exams by the oncologist; mental by her short term memory improving; mentally by her depression being much less and she expressed in many ways a strong will to live; and spiritually by returning to choir this coming Wednesday. She stated she is praying more. Sometimes, even with all the recent progress I feel small and insignificant to deal with all of this. Thankfully I have God and Joy and all of my family, my biological family and my family of friends all over the world to help keep me loving and focused one-day-at-a-time. I am finding that the "Dark Night of the Soul" written about so well by St. John of the Cross and others can be experienced in brief snippets in a single day or over an extended period of time. I believe that God does not move, but sometimes I do. Thankfully these short moves away from God by me are shorter and shorter all the time. My response to God is not a one-time settled thing. Goodnight and sleep well.

September 26, 2012   by Joy Pentz: We got the MRI report, and it looks better than the rough estimate Fri right after the MRI. Her tumor has shrunk 80% in volume since May. It is right next to her brainstem, but not in it. Please keep praying because she is not out of the woods by any means YET. Miraculous! Joy

> *Comment by Joy, January 3, 2018: Apparently, I had not done the calculations correctly for any of these shrinkage reports, and these numbers are way off. The important thing is that the tumor was not growing.*

September 26, 2012 by Marty Pentz. I need to say this again, Elise's tumor is 80% smaller than it was in May and is out of her brainstem. She started another five day round of chemo last night and had some nausea today and has been quite tired, exhausted actually. This stuff is tiring and tough on her, but is killing this tumor. She told me the other day her will to live is strong and I had the impression she wants to fight this cancer with all she has. She is doing all she can to get better. Monday night when she called me for a ride she sounded like the Elise of 18 months ago. I could not stop smiling. After her oncology appointment and Avastin drip we went to the Neuro ICU where she spent three weeks in May and at that time we had some doctors telling us she would not make it. The nurses all remembered her and appeared to be in awe of her recovery. That was such a tough time and Joy and I often wonder how we got through all of it. We did it one-day-at-a-time with God, prayer, numerous visits from many of you, meals many of you brought, phone calls and Love, Love, Love. What a journey. I am going on a three-day silent Ignatian retreat this weekend. I am really looking forward to this time alone with God. "Act as if everything depended on you; trust as if everything depended on God." St. Ignatius of Loyola

September 28, 2012 by Marty Pentz: I wrote this last night, but then had computer problems 2259 hours the 27th of September 2012. Elise told me tonight she is glad she is clean and is also glad she is alive and wants to live. I have been unable to sleep on this eve of my attending the Ignatian silent retreat. At times silence seems to draw me into it. This will be my 6th or 7th silent Jesuit retreat. The effects on me have been from the profound to the very subtle, but they have all moved me along this spiritual journey we are all on. I have some anxiety about leaving Elise, but Joy can handle all this for now. We have developed a routine that makes all this medicine, doctors' appointments, therapy and all the rest as doable, and with no more stress than is necessary. Keep praying. This is a version of the five-step Daily Examen that St. Ignatius practiced. Become aware of God's presence. Review the day with gratitude. Pay attention to your emotions. "Choose one feature of the day and pray from it. Look toward tomorrow." This is what I work to do daily and on these retreats.

September 30, 2012 by Marty Pentz, 2142 hours. Got back from the Ignatian silent retreat this past weekend and found God in my need to cut the grass. I have come to like the simple chores in life. Elise said today she really likes her life. We keep going forward a day at a time. When Elise was diagnosed with a malignant brain tumor, my life changed drastically in a heartbeat, but God was there. I will keep praying for what I am to do next.

October 5, 2012 by Joy Pentz. Elise is doing so well. We had a family meeting with the rehab therapists, and they are very pleased with her progress. They think she is ready to take a class or two. That is a goal Elise set for herself, but she feels overwhelmed when she thinks about actually doing it. They said she should start doing more things at home like dishes and cleaning her room. We like that idea. They said she is not ready to drive because she doesn't always attend to things on the left side since her tumor is on the right, and driving requires lots of attention to the left. I said I guess she might have to move to England to drive. The other thing she has to work on is prosody, which has to do with the inflection of her voice and facial expressions. Right side brain injuries in the area of her tumor cause that problem. Her voice is rather monotone and she has a flat affect. I suggested she exaggerate her inflection and expression, and it will look normal to other people. I also said she should observe and imitate others. For example, people usually raise their eyebrows when they greet others, so now she does that in a silly way to joke with me. She has become so loving towards me and calls me Mommy. I hugged her today and told her how happy I am she is back with us, and she said thanks for not killing me, referring to some of the doctors' advice not to start or keep her on life support. I told her I kept begging her to come back to us. She said she listened to me. Actually she has no memory of hearing anything, and she didn't have a near death out of body experience. I don't know how we got through that time. I chose to believe she would be ok because the alternative was unthinkable to me. All of your messages and prayers have meant so much to us. Joy

October 6, 2012 by Marty Pentz, 1747 hours. The benefits of silent retreats always linger for me. This has been a very reflective, emotional and peaceful week. Elise continues to improve and has asserted that she is very glad to be alive. Her emotions have come back and she is re-learning how to express them. The human brain is such an interesting organ.

0756 hours the 7 October 2012. As I was saying about the human brain and its amazing properties and weirdness, Elise has issues with left sided awareness. She can use her left side and is, but at times will "forget" what is over on that side. She felt overwhelmed earlier this week as her life gets busier again. After discussing goals moving forward we (we means Elise, Joy, myself and prayer) decided that for now she will concentrate on her various forms of rehab and add more as time goes on. As much as she looks and talks like the Elise of old, and how smart she is, I at times can forget the impact this tumor had and is still having on her brain. She wants to go back to school so she is thinking of taking one class in the spring. She will be done with the four day per week rehab by then and be in regular outpatient rehab so will need something to do. For some reason this week my brain has been going back to that day in May when we had to call 911 and take her to the hospital by ambulance. Time for me to go sing and will finish this later today.

1507 hours the same day. It was good to sing sacred Anglican music today. I am sitting here watching football and baseball with Elise sleeping on the couch and Joy is at orchestra practice where she plays the violin. Music is so important to our healing and lives. As an aside, I love what I do for a living. "If a man is engaged in his proper work he attains the highest end." from Hinduism" And from Confucianism, "When you know a thing, to recognize that you know it, and when you do not know a thing, to recognize that you do not know it – that is knowledge."

October 9, 2012 by Joy Pentz. Elise is about to be hooked up to her Avastin drip at the doctor's office. All of her blood work and vital signs are fine. She told the doc her mood is at 1 on a scale of 1-10, with 10 being the worst, and that she wants to live. She was able to take a standup shower by herself. She met her goal for walking up to speed. She went to St Monica for personal healing and group meditation Sunday. She started tying a knot in a piece of yarn for each cigarette she smokes, and this is helping her to keep her smoking to 1/2 pack per day. It's better than making marks on her hand and she doesn't have to find a pen each time and it doesn't wash off. She is actually cutting the yarn each day and keeping track of it in her pocket.

October 9, 2012 by Marty Pentz, 2313 hours. This has been an interesting day off. I have been thinking a lot about life lately, as one would expect, and not only this recent time with Elise's brain tumor, but earlier spiritual experiences throughout my whole life. Listening to the locked out Indianapolis Symphony Musicians play Beethoven's fifth piano concerto and two other pieces last night was a two hour smile. I have shared a number of the times I have been moved by God since this experience with Elise began. I have been looking back at other times in my life, especially since I got sober that I was touched by God. Seeing the waterfalls and other vistas while hiking in the Smokey Mountains a couple of years ago. I felt God's presence when I was walking Emily down the aisle to marry Matthew in this old Anglican Church in England. Walking Emily down the aisle and being in that place of worship I felt the presence of God. More on this later. Elise wants to live and she is now angry at the cancer. She is fighting hard and we move forward by the day from here. I also watched the Indiana Fever win a WNBA playoff game, shot at the buzzer to win, to extend this round one more game. My most beneficial healthy escapes from cancer, although I do not believe I am ever completely away, are time with Joy, Elise, Skyping with Emily and Lilia and Matthew, attending symphonies, sporting events and other activities. I love and appreciate all the love showered on Elise and all of us in so many forms.

1840 hours the 9th of October 2012 by Marty Pentz. Elise is planning to go on a retreat this weekend; this will be good for her and all of us. She is getting back into her life. There is a lot going on in my heart and soul, but I am unsure how to write about this. I have a reverence for the music I sing at church and the psalms we sing. I love that Trinity Episcopal is involved in so many different ministries to numerous populations of people. I also have a bachelor's degree in the scholastic study of world religions and have gained much from all that I have studied and experienced. I feel I have a personal relationship with God, which grows closer day-by-day, but could not honestly put this relationship in any religious box. I simply know that I love God, praying, worship, singing, service and that this is all possible due to many years of active recovery from addictions. Thank you all for reading what I write and your feedback on how this is impacting your lives. This means a lot to me.

October 11, 2012 by Marty Pentz: Elise is going on a "Heart to Heart" retreat this weekend for woman in any type of recovery program for addictions or related to those with addictions. This will be the first time since last December 10th (ten months ago) she has been able to be without Joy, myself or Drew for any length of time. This is a big step for Elise and for us. Joy and I will be home by ourselves this weekend. I am singing a lot this weekend. We have three hour rehearsal on Saturday, service on Sunday morning and the Three Choir Evensong with two other Episcopal churches on Meridian Street in Indy. I cannot wait. I will continue this tomorrow night.

2027 hours the 11th of October 2012. I received a text from Elise today where she stated she had run for five minutes. What a miraculous recovery from being on a ventilator in May. I was reminded today of the loneliness of a person in the throes of addiction. The beginnings of recovery from addiction can be frightening. The love all of you have given Elise and all of us is an example to me of seeing God in the world. I see one of my purposes in life as a conduit of all the love I receive from you all and God so I can be of service to my family and those I work with in the fellowship I belong to and at the VA. I sang Psalm 25 tonight and here are some of the words that touched me: A Prayer for Guidance, Pardon and Protection, a Psalm of

David. "Unto thee, O LORD, do I lift up my soul. O my God, I trust in Thee. Let me not be ashamed, let not mine enemies triumph over me. Yea, let none that wait on thee be ashamed. Let them be ashamed which transgress without cause. Show me thy ways, O LORD; teach me thy paths. Lead me in thy truth, and teach me: for thou art the God of my salvation; on thee do I wait all the day.

October 13, 2012 by Joy Pentz. Elise is at her women's retreat. She went with a friend, who is also going to make sure she takes her meds. Yesterday her brain injury rehab group took a field trip to Barnes and Noble. The purpose of the field trips is community re-entry. When they were discussing the trip the day before in group, she suggested they do a type of scavenger hunt. The occupational therapist had her write the instructions for each member of the group according to their abilities. There are a handful of patients in the group, most of whom are older stroke survivors. The scavenger hunt items ranged from just walking to the information desk to asking for a particular book and then finding it on the shelf. For example, one she wrote for herself was to ask for a book about pencil and ink drawing and then buy it. We were quite impressed with her creative idea and ability to tailor the lists to the abilities of her fellow patients. Even though she is the only brain tumor patient, and the only very young person, she forms bonds with those who join the group. They have graduation parties with the patient's family when they transition out of group. So far the only other patient who did not have a stroke was a young police officer with a gunshot wound to his head, but he graduated and is back at work at a desk job. It's nice to see instances where employers provide reasonable accommodations; naturally we at EEOC deal with those whose employers have not done so since we enforce the Americans with Disabilities Act.

Yesterday one of the speech therapists who worked with Elise when she was at Hook rehab as an inpatient filled in for her outpatient speech therapist, and was amazed at her progress. Of course we loved hearing that. I can't wait to see Elise's progress with prosody because it is difficult to imagine she is no longer depressed and indifferent about survival when her flat affect and monotone voice make her come across that way. I don't want to bug her asking about that, but once in a while I need to hear it from her in words to believe it. Actually I don't think she has ever been happier or more excited about life, another gift (besides growing closer to us) of what she now refers to as f---ing cancer. I don't ask her to not use that word with me because it is so good to hear she is fighting against it in her spirit.

October 14, 2012 by Joy Pentz. I am so grateful for all of your messages of support and your prayers. This is sometimes a very lonely experience I love it when you ask about Elise, and when I start to tell you the latest you already know about it from here. When I started this I just wanted to have one place to update people. I had no idea it would be inspirational to people or that we would share so much private information (by we, I mean Marty). I have always wanted to keep my different worlds separate like George on Seinfeld. I felt like they would collide, especially work and personal. Well, they did collide, but instead of exploding into smithereens, they melded into a bigger family. I can no longer retreat to the invisible anonymous self I feel most comfortable as. Letting others in a bit more is very comforting.

One of the things Elise is working on is developing a better filter between her brain and her mouth. She no longer tells her physical therapist what she needs to do when she goes to the restroom. She just excuses herself and tells her where she is going. It's amazing the little things that are affected depending on where the tumor is. I'm just saying...I'm not going to get that personal with you, don't worry.

I am so happy Elise is having a good time at the retreat. She has sent us several texts and called to tell us the things she is excited about. She climbed a rock wall and went on a zip line. She posted a picture of it on fb. She texted to say they were about to do a sing along. I wrote back, that's your true love, and she said yes ma'am. She loves sharing her accomplishments with us now.

When Elise went to Spain a few years ago she posted a picture of herself jumping into the sea from a quite high cliff with other kids. I was so glad I didn't know about it ahead of time, and only found out after she was safe. It gave meaning to the question parents ask, "So if all your friends were jumping off a cliff, would you want to do that too?" For Elise the answer is yes ma'am. I have been taking Elise to a Sunday morning meditation meeting, which has been wonderful for both of us. I need to get ready for that now. I decided I didn't have to miss out just because Elise is not here. I find it so difficult to get myself to sit still to meditate even though I know it is so helpful to me. At least I know I will do it for a short time each week if I go to this meeting

October 14, 2012 by Marty Pentz, 2030 hours. This has been an amazing weekend. Those of you that are Facebook friends with Elise know she went on a women's retreat this weekend and had a ball. On top of the spiritual and emotional focus of this Heart to Heart weekend, Elise climbed a rock wall and rode down a zip line. This is the same young lady who was on a ventilator and trach just this past May. Miracles keep happening. I had the honor and the pleasure of singing all weekend. Trinity choir sang with Christ Church Cathedral and St. Paul's Cathedral in a three choir Evensong. We had a three hour choir rehearsal on Saturday, sang our normal mass at our church this morning, had another three choir rehearsal for another hour and then sang the Evensong at 4pm. It was glorious, I simply love singing to God and everybody else. Elise is better all the time. "Out of difficulties grow miracles." Jean de laBruyere

October 16, 2012 by Marty Pentz, 1934 hours. While Elise is doing so well and liking her life, there are days where I still get so angry that she has brain cancer. This has been one of those days. After talking with Elise tonight I am feeling better about all of this. It does not help that I have not been feeling very well today. When I remember that God is with Elise and all of us and has and is healing her I find ways to see much joy in my life. I have had many people share with me that my spiritual journey through all of this has been a help and an inspiration to them. I feel blessed that God has used our pain, despair and joy for benefit. All the love is such a blessing. "Though our feelings come and go, God's love for us does not." C.S. Lewis

October 18, 2012 by Joy Pentz. I have been anxious about Elise the last few days because she has been restless and antsy. We tried omitting her 2nd dose of Ritalin, but without it she has to take an afternoon nap, which doesn't work on therapy days. She only takes 5 mg twice a day. I felt better that omitting the second dose on a non-therapy day relieved some of her restlessness. It's hard not to think of any change as being caused by tumor growth. She seems more tired than usual even with the second dose, but she is fighting a cold and probably catching up on rest from the retreat. She also said she needs glasses, so of course I am worried that the tumor has grown close to her optic nerve again. She has her next MRI in November. All I can do is pray and choose to believe. I frequently look at clinical trials and developments because tumor regrowth is common. I found info about an FDA approved method to destroy tumors in soft tissue using tiny probes to deliver short bursts of electrical pulses guided by MRI. It has been used successfully on tumors outside the brain in humans and on brain tumors in dogs. I would think a neurosurgeon skilled in laser ablation could do this as well. A modified version of this method has also been used to deliver chemotherapy directly to tumors and around the margins. Another clinical trial I found uses a drug that synchronizes the replication of tumor cells so that all the cancer cells are in the optimal stage when Temodar is used 5 days per month. The other hope is the explosion of medical advances based on the human genome and vaccinations using the patient's own tumor cells and blood. The problem with clinical trials is you have to qualify, and if you don't you have to wait for FDA approval and hope it comes on time. Most of the clinical trials for Elise's type of tumor are for grade 4, and hers is grade 3. When I get scared it helps to remind myself of all the possibilities in mainstream and alternative medicine. Elise is not only saying she wants to live, she is saying she is going to live.

From Marty. October 22, 2012, 2337 hours. The Indiana Fever just won the WNBA Championship. It has been so much fun being at all these games, thanks to Todd, who is Drew's father, and a physical therapist for the team. Elise has a cold and a cough, but otherwise is doing really well. This is her week of chemo and she sees the oncology Dr. on Tuesday. Do not know how her cold impacts whether or not she gets chemo, but we will find out Tuesday. She really loves life these days. A friend of mine had a vigil service for her at his church on Saturday and the mass was excellent. We chose not to go to the Merry Widow today. With Elise's compromised immune system we did not want to expose her to so many possible germs. We will go to a local opera or some other dad/daughter outing later. The leaves in our whole neighborhood are a beautiful golden color and all over the ground and still in the trees. This part of God's beauty is simply awesome. I found gratitude in the Fever championship win, God's beauty, lovely walk with Joy and Elise saying I love you. I saw God in many places today. There was beauty in this well played basketball game. "Though we travel the world over to find the beautiful, we must carry it with us or we find it not. ~Ralph Waldo Emerson" I also saw the beauty in Elise's smile today and her saying I love you. "Beauty is not in the face; beauty is a light in the heart. ~Kahlil Gibran"

October 25, 2012, by Marty Pentz, 2122 hours. I have not written in a few days and have been reflecting a lot today. Tomorrow would have been my dad's 89th birthday; he died three years ago yesterday. Elise is doing very well and her symptoms related to the cancer keep getting better and better. She was diagnosed yesterday with shingles so she is taking even more meds for a time as this week is chemo week as well. We will love through this as well. I have talked in the past about this Ignatian stuff I have been doing. I am in the process of a thirty day retreat in daily life. I end my day now with what is called an Examen and comprises the following: "1. I recall that I am in the presence of God. 2. I then spend a moment looking over my day with gratitude for this day's gifts. 3. I then ask God to help me look at my actions and attitudes and motives with honesty and patience. 4. I then review my day. And finally, 5. What can I do better tomorrow? This exercise has helped to wake up with gratitude in my heart and to live more of each day with gratitude and understanding

October 30, 2012 by Joy Pentz: Elise's shingles are no longer contagious, so she can get back to her therapy, which she calls adult day camp. Fortunately Drew noticed her rash right away, and I recognized it as shingles having seen it on a family member before. Since she got on anti-viral meds right away, she had a very mild case. I have added to my prayers all the people affected by Hurricane Sandy and its aftermath. It makes any problems I have seem small with the exception of Elise's health. In speech therapy Elise is writing a research paper. She chose the topic of the effect of piracy on the music industry. We were looking at the website of Stupid Cancer.org, which was started for young adults by a brain cancer survivor who was diagnosed 16 years ago. They are going to have a get together in Las Vegas in Apr, and Elise is excited about the prospect of attending. She would also like to make contact before then with others her age battling cancer. She has not met any other brain cancer patients, or patients her age with any type of cancer. The brain injured people she is with in rehab are older stroke patients or victims of accidents. On the stupid cancer website there is a link to a talk radio blog. You can do a live show with listeners calling in and you can turn the show into a podcast. We did one in which I interviewed her about her cancer experience. I hope she is up for doing another one because we can do a better job of it. If she wants to do a call in show I will ask her to post it beforehand so you can call in if you want. To the extent I can enjoy the moment and not project into the future with worry, I can be happy and appreciate her miraculous comeback. It is not only that she was able to get off life support and regain consciousness, but also that her functioning is so much better than any time since her diagnosis in December. Thanks so much for your continued prayers and messages.

November 1, 2012 by Marty Pentz, 2007 hours. I have not written in a while and need to talk to all of you. I feel blessed that Elise has been able to stay on our insurance as she would possibly not be here and we would certainly be bankrupt. That is enough said on the financial end of this whole cancer thing. Our delightful daughter is slowly returning to herself and becoming more. Loving. She has always been a loving person, but now she shows it more. Tomorrow night Elise, three of my good friends and I are going to dinner and then to see the Indianapolis Symphony and the Indianapolis Symphonic Choir perform the Brahms German Requiem. I am looking forward to this. Elise and I are going to vote this Saturday as well. I ran into two friends at Target tonight, one a social work colleague from the VA and the other from the fellowship I belong to. I had just dropped Elise off at a meeting and was feeling kind of bummed at how fatigued she is by the combination of the medical and emotional side of this cancer and seeing these two people from separate parts of my world picked me up and was a blessing. With a tumor, chemo, rehab, fear, and months in hospitals it is expected for her to be quite fatigued. It is still difficult to see my vibrant and beautiful 20-year old daughter so tired so often. She said she has good energy and feels quite well in the mornings, but by afternoon is tired. We are planning a Thanksgiving trip to MN and cannot wait. During my evening prayer and meditation time I look for the beauty in my day since I woke up. Looking for where I could see God. Today I heard beauty in Elise chuckling, I saw beauty in helping a veteran get the long-term inpatient treatment needed, I saw beauty in my two friends I ran into in Target, wondrous beauty in looking at my granddaughter Lilia's picture, and in hearing Joy's voice when she called me today. This quote is how I like to live in this world. "A man should hear a little music, read a little poetry, and see a fine picture every day of his life, in order that worldly cares may not obliterate the sense of the beautiful which God has implanted in the human soul." Johann Wolfgang von Goethe

November 4, 2012 by Marty Pentz, 2245 hours. This has been a good and difficult day, as many have been lately. Elise ran for 8 minutes at rehab today and she and I went to dinner with some good friends of mine. We then went to the symphony and she was only able to stay until intermission due to fatigue. At times like that I get so angry at the cancer and underneath the anger is fear. I do not remember the future being so scary. Most of the time I do not look there and I am very able to stay much focused the day I am in. Sleep is not coming easy tonight. Joy is scared and angry as well. I will love and focus on now. I will write more tomorrow.

2239 hours the 4th of November 2012. I missed a day of writing. Another night of struggling to sleep. Last night Joy, Elise, Drew and I went to a banquet of a fellowship most of us belong to and the dinner, fellowship and speaker were all good. Elise's thinking appears to be getting better all the time. We are working crossword puzzles with her and she is doing very well. She also does them by herself when she is out on the deck smoking, and can do them well. She sang along with some Sound of Music at Joy's concert today and she stated it made her feel better. We are going to get her to sing more on a daily basis. Any of you that can get her to sing more the better her mood will be. She has been kind of down the past few days. She had a real zest for life two weeks ago and that momentum has dissipated. Lying here in bed and not sleeping I was getting fearful. Writing to you all I am feeling more hopeful again. She hardly uses her left hand and that is not getting better. I will push that some. Even with my strong faith in God as her Healer I can get very afraid. Humility is certainly one value I am often confronted with in recent years, if not most of my years. God is there as well. I am blessed to have a loving God in my life.

11/5/12 From Joy Pentz: Here is today's radiologist's report: FULL RESULT: Indication: Anaplastic astrocytoma.   Comparison: Multiple prior studies extending to December 10, 2011.   Findings: Note is made of a hemorrhagic mass centered within the right thalamus measuring 3.5 x 2.8 x 2.5 cm. This demonstrates mass effect upon the adjacent third ventricle. The mass measured 3.8 x 3.0 cm on September 21, 2012. The mass measured 4.5 x 3.3 cm on July 26, 2012. The mass measured 4.8 x 4.5 cm on May 5, 2012. There is peripheral hemosiderin staining and signal characteristic of old and late subacute blood products. Again noted is T2 hyperintensity radiating into the corona radiata of the right parietal lobe posterior to the mass. Mass demonstrates restricted diffusion. This is due to the blood products. This may represent retrograde Wallerian degeneration. There is a left transfrontal ventricular catheter coursing through the anterior frontal horns. The lateral ventricles are normal in size. Again noted is a pachymeningeal enhancement over the cerebral hemispheres. This is likely reactive from the shunt. Flow-voids of the large intracranial arteries are normal. Marrow signal is normal. The mastoid air cells and paranasal sinuses are clear.   IMPRESSION: There is a gradual decrease in size of the right thalamic mass demonstrating regions of mineralization and blood products. Continued follow up is recommended. Findings may indicate a treatment response.   ELECTRONICALLY SIGNED BY: B, M.D. Nov 5 2012 8:00PM

November 6, 2012 by Joy Pentz.   Elise and I are at the doctor's office waiting for her Avastin drip. We were very frightened yesterday. The nurse that comes once a week to change the dressing on Elise's PICC line noticed that Elise was holding her left hand like she used to-- balled up and against her waist, and she had noticed it for the first time last week, but not so tightly balled up. Also she has been depressed and more tired than usual. The nurse called the doctor, and the doctor sent us to the ER for an MRI. Thank God the tumor has not progressed, and she had not had a stroke or bleed. Her doctor said her strength is the same, and she saw no neurological changes. We are chalking up her recent symptoms to her meds for Shingles and missing therapy and just hanging around the house until she was not contagious anymore.

While we were waiting for the results, even though I am always keeping up with clinical trials and new research in case the chemo she is on stops working, I still felt lost about what to do next. It is much different to look in the abstract just in case as opposed to the reality of finding an open clinical trial she qualifies for that works logistically right at the time you need it. Dr. Jessica asked Elise if there was any way she would think about quitting smoking. She said if she just had one wish for Hanukkah /Christmas it would be that. I said really you would use your one wish on that? She said, I love Elise. She said she is really invested in her, and she is doing so much better than she would have ever believed possible in May. I told her we feel like Elise is her only patient the way she treats her.

On Sunday Elise went to the nursing home where the community orchestra I am in was performing. She sang to the medley of the Sound of Music, and got the people at her table singing also. Singing completely changes her frame of mind. I have suggested that she sing first thing in the morning to start her day on a happy note. I have started playing a piece on the violin each morning, and it gets me humming. I am usually cranky and not wanting to get out of bed, and that transforms my mood. I used to do it if I had time after getting ready, but it works much better if I do it first.

The nurse just came in with a gift from the little wish foundation, an iPod Touch with a $50 gift card to the App Store. It's not worth getting cancer for of course, but still very nice. Thanks again for all your prayers and messages. They mean the world to us.

November 6, 2012 by Joy Pentz. Great news! I learned this morning that the profusion images from the MRI showed no profusion. That means there are no visible blood vessels feeding the tumor, so it is very possible the tumor is dead. Ding dong the witch is dead, the wicked witch is dead! (Hopefully)

November 6, 2012   by Marty Pentz, 2030 hours the 6th of November 2012. The miracle continues. Yesterday the nurse that sees Elise every Monday was concerned that her left hand was getting more and more constricted. The nurse told Elise's doctor about her concerns and then Dr. Jessica ordered an emergency MRI. The fear of her tumor being worse was great. The tumor is 30% smaller than it was a month ago and there is no visible blood supply to the tumor. Everything is working. She looks like Elise again and is so loving and caring. Emily, Lilia and Matthew will be here in December and Daniel and Sara as well. Last December 10th when we found out Elise had a tumor our lives and those holidays changed. We are going to Minnesota for Thanksgiving. While staying one-day-at-a-time, this coming holiday season promises to be much different than last year. In choir a few weeks ago we sang a song entitled "What Wondrous Love is This" and the following line keeps running through my mind and soul, "What wondrous love is this, O my soul, O my soul." My love of God keeps growing and growing. I cannot stop smiling.

ELISE HUGGING AND KISSING HER DAD, WHO IS ABOUT TO SING IN THE CHOIR

November 7, 2012 by Joy Pentz: What a relief. Elise would not be alive today without good insurance coverage. She was diagnosed at age 19, and she had to withdraw from college because her health made it impossible to remain a full time college student. Without health care reform those two facts would mean she would no longer be covered by our insurance. We are so grateful.

November 18, 2012, by Marty Pentz. I have wanted to write in the past week, but for whatever reason I could not get myself to write. Elise is doing really well, the tumor keeps shrinking and it appears to be dead. My and our lives are getting to a new equilibrium. There is a lot of joy in my life. My love for Joy continues to be boundless, Daniel is engaged to be married, Emily has a beautiful daughter and God and medicine are healing and saving Elise. All will be here for Christmas.

1348 hours the 18th of November 2012. I was too tired to finish last night. We are going to see the movie "Flight" in a few minutes so may not finish now either. At different times in my life I have been more or less an active person. Lately, I find myself more contemplative and pray and meditate and read a lot. I am drawn to the writings of those that are considered mystics or books about mysticism. The novels I am likely to read are science fiction and/or fantasy. I like novels that have at least a hint of spirituality in them and the fight between good and evil is not always clear, as in life. Part of my evening prayer time is spent in seeing where I could see beauty and love in the day just past, what Saint Ignatius might call seeing God in all things. I am going to end my musings today with a quote from a rather strange, but interesting book that Elise gave me some time ago called "Odd Apocalypse" by Dean Koontz (p. 15): "We are all the walking wounded in a world that is a war zone. Everything we love will be taken from us, everything, last of all life itself. Yet everywhere I look. I find great beauty in this battlefield, and grace and the promise of joy."

December 2, 2012 by Marty Pentz, 2113 hours. I have not written in a while and need to. I attended a workshop yesterday on memoir writing. I plan on writing the story of the past year or two in some fashion. Elise and I have been singing in the car the past couple of days with the following songs the highlights: Billie Jean, Thriller, American Pie, and Time in a Bottle. She is doing really well. I am looking forward to all the family that is coming for the holidays. Emily, Matthew and Lilia, Daniel and Sara, Joy's sisters and their kids, my sister Kaye and possibly Joy's brothers' daughter Amanda. My spirit feels buoyant tonight. Eternity is today. I am tired and time for bed, goodnight.

December 8, 2012 by Joy Pentz: Elise signed up for a class at IUPUI to continue to work towards a degree. She emailed the prof to see if the econ class she wants has much math, and it's just arithmetic so she is taking it. She has an eye doctor appointment so she can get glasses and drive. It will be a year Monday since we found out about her tumor, and she is better than she has ever been since the months before her diagnosis. What a journey this has been this past year. Your support has made all the difference. Elise says she is almost glad for the cancer because it has made her believe in God and brought her closer to us. She never realized how much love was all around her. Thank God for this miracle.

December 8, 2012 by Joy Pentz. We just got back from Man of La Mancha at Mud Creek Players. It was great. Elise filled out a form to be on their mailing list and the person she gave it to invited her to stay for the party after the play because she said she was interested in getting involved as an actress. She was sitting between us and put her arms around both of us during the play. She kissed me on the cheek and said "I love you Mommy" I told her I don't think I have ever been happier in my life. She said she hasn't either. Last week Elise gave a lead and shared her recovery story at my meeting for family and friends of addicts. It was so quiet you could hear a pin drop. Then one of the members shared how it has affected her to be a witness to Elise's miracle through Caring Bridge, and she got teary. Then all of a sudden almost everyone, about 30 people, started crying, and Kleenex was being passed around the circle to everybody. Elise thanked me for the experience.

When she was in the hospital, I kept encouraging her when she was so afraid she would not be able to go back to college, by telling her she could be a motivational speaker by talking about her recovery from addiction and brain cancer. She could incorporate her humor and desire to make people laugh. I also suggested she write a book about her story because she is such a good writer. She has so much to share and so many great things ahead of her whatever she decides she wants and is able to do. I feel so grateful for this joyful time with Elise that I never expected to experience. It feels like Marty and I have been through hell these last 5 years with Elise, but it was all leading up to this slice of heaven with her.

December 10, 2012 by Marty Pentz, 2042 hours. Today marks a year since we found out that Elise has a brain tumor. What a year this has been. Along with all the anguish and fear there have been many blessings. The main blessing is she is still with us and getting better all the time. God has been good to us in all the love from all of you out there. I feel closer to God. I did not think it was possible, but I love my family more than ever. I am really looking forward to everybody being here for Christmas. I saw beauty today in talking with Joy about our sometimes ongoing fear. There was beauty in the laughter I shared with a couple of colleagues at work today. God is in everything and the Spirit is with me today.

ONE YEAR SINCE TUMOR FOUND   December 10, 2012   Hello all, this is Elise! I'm so grateful to be alive today. And it's been a whole year since we found my tumor (though it feels like much longer to me). I'm just so grateful for this time with my mom and all of the love I've realized is in my life. Sometimes it takes the hard times to really realize how blessed we are. I truly have the best parents and the best boyfriend in the world. Thank you God! And I actually believe in God now. Thank you so much for all your encouragement and tribute donations in my name, I feel honored to have such a following. And thank you for your prayers, they seem to be working!

January 3, 2013 by Joy Pentz: Just a note to thank all of you for all your support and to update you. Elise seems to be getting better all the time. She continues to have normal blood counts, and no noticeable side effects from chemo. She is still tired and sleepy, but even that seems to be improving. She is on a very low dose of Ritalin, 5 Mg twice a day, to help with staying alert and awake. Most days she doesn't take her second dose, and still continues her normal activities until a normal bedtime with her usual naps. She got glasses yesterday, and will take her road test Monday so she will be cleared for driving. She has already passed all the tests for reaction time and attentiveness etc. that brain injured patients must be evaluated for. Her main problem was left inattentiveness from having a right sided tumor.

Elise had her graduation celebration from rehab Friday. One of the comments was remembering how Elise always turned right no matter where she was going. Good thing the rehab hallways circle the rooms so she would get to her destination eventually anyway. I initially thought she had lost her keen sense of direction, but even when she always turned right she was able to direct her directionally challenged mother as a passenger. Elise is still less animated in facial expressions and intonation, but improving. I have to remind myself that her mood is not reflected in her face. Otherwise I think she is an angry sullen teenager. It helps me to ask her to smile and to tell her I love her because her responses are not angry and sullen, and she has not been a teenager for 10 months.

It does me so much good to watch a funny show with her to hear her laugh. Her wit and dry humor are back, and she can joke and tease with a straight face now. She hardly ever needs to be reminded to use her filter now. She asked three of her health care workers if they were gay before developing a better filter between her thoughts and her speech. Although she sometimes has short term memory lapses, for the most part her memory is amazing. If you did not know her before her tumor, you would not know anything was wrong with her.

Marty took her to IUPUI this morning to speak to a guidance counselor and enrolled her in a class or two. They will also go to the disability office to ask for reasonable accommodations for test taking. The rehab suggested she ask to have a non-distracting setting and more time for tests. She was going to audit some extra classes, but that costs the same as tuition, so we will find other avenues where she can pursue her interests in singing, acting, drawing and computer graphic arts. She is also going to apply to be a volunteer at Riley Children's Hospital, which is on campus. She is working to strike a balance between staying busy with constructive activities, finding time to get enough rest and not getting stressed out or overwhelmed now that she is no longer in full day rehab.

Today is the last day of Emily, Matthew and Lilia's visit. Lilia is 5 months old and so smiley and delightful. I love being a grandma. We also got to meet Daniel's fiancé, Sara, and we all like her very much. My sister, Carol, and her son, Aaron, were here, and that was wonderful as well. My other sister, Doreen, and her daughters, Lauren and Hannah, were not able to come due to road conditions and because she is needed to help my dad with my mom, who fell and broke her shoulder. Thank you Doreen! We are all so grateful for all your support, prayers and messages. Please continue praying for Elise's defeat of cancer. Thank you and best wishes to all of you in the New Year.

January 3, 2013 by Marty Pentz, 1653 hours. I have not written in this forum in quite some time. I have been writing in my journal, but for some reason I have not been able to get myself to write to you all. As you might expect my emotions have been up and down, mostly up. Emily, Matthew and Lilia will be here for another few days. Lilia is so wonderful and beautiful, she is five months old. Daniel and his fiancée Sara were here for a few days over Christmas. She is a delightful and beautiful person. Joy and I both feel blessed that all three of our kids have somebody in their lives to love and to love them. Love is really all there is to make a good life. "Being deeply loved by someone gives you strength, while loving someone deeply gives you courage." Lao Tzu.

ELISE WITH HER FIRST NIECE, LILIA

1935 hours the 3rd of January 2013 by Marty Pentz. We just had probably the best three weeks of our life. Daniel and Sara were here. Emily, Matthew and wondrous baby Lilia have been here for close to three weeks and sadly are leaving for home tomorrow. Elise is doing very well and is starting one class next week and is taking her driving test on Monday to see if she can drive again. And to think she was close to dying last May. Joy's sister Carol and her son Aaron were here as well. All in all an amazing holiday. I have been reading numerous memoirs as part of my training to write my own in the near future. The one I am currently reading is by the man who taught the memoir writing workshop I recently attended. His name is Jim McGarrah and the book is entitled "A Temporary Sort of Peace." A quote from this book describing an aspect of Marine Corp basic training, as he looked back over many years, I found quite profound: "The art of living, as distinguished from just existing, lies in the ability to be different, to grow and change, evolve into something greater than the sum of its parts. When everyone looks and acts the same, the beauty of humanity can often become a beast. A burr haircut begins the descent." I feel called to contribute what I can on a daily basis to the love and peace in the world.

January 10, 2013 by Marty Pentz, 2151 hours. As well as Elise is doing there are times in any given day where I am gripped by fear. Then I remember that God is fully with us all and the fear diminishes. Then with gratitude I can look at where she was last May and that she is taking a micro economics class in college today. I am helped by limiting the thinking I do about the tumor, other than praying for shrinkage, and focus on loving all that I can. I find that I am noticing more and more beauty in the world and people caring for each other. For the most part I have stopped watching news programs. There is nothing there for me. Over the years, especially the last one, I have learned that to have peace I need to read more and more on others journey of faith and recovery. I have been reading memoirs of others that in some aspect of life have been through the emotional ringer. They give me much hope and are helping me to learn how to write my own stories leading to a memoir. Reading these memoirs, praying and meditating, seeing the beauty in each day and sharing in the Fellowship I belong to are all helping me to find my voice. I love my life with Joy. We are reading a book together on hope written by a breast cancer survivor. Joy is reading it with Elise as well. "The very least you can do in your life is figure out what you hope for. And the most you can do is live inside that hope. Not admire it from a distance but live right in it, under its roof." Barbara Kingsolver, "The world is indeed full of peril and in it there are many dark places. But still there is much that is fair. And though in all lands, love is now mingled with grief, it still grows, perhaps, the greater." J.R.R. Tolkien, The Lord of the Rings

January 11, 2013 by Marty Pentz, 1957 hours. When I was in high school I once had dinner with a friend that had 11 siblings. One was adopted. I asked her mother how she had enough love for all her kids and she said, to her, love does not need to be split between each kid, that with each new child her love multiplies. When I first stopped drinking many years ago and was married to my first wife I did not think I had the ability to feel normal emotions. I was learning to treat people well, but did not feel anything that felt at all like love. All I had access to was anger. I did not know I was so afraid of intimacy and letting people know me. I will not go into it here what went into the decision to shut myself down emotionally, just need to say that I did and alcohol helped. After getting divorced, through the process of inventory and therapy I started to wake up emotionally. I did not wake up pretty. When I started to wake up emotionally, for a time I could not stop crying. I am now usually emotionally present, even when it is hard. This past year with Elise and cancer I have felt it all. Intense fear and anger while at times almost unbelievable joy in her return to us. Waking up emotionally has helped me to be aware of the presence of God in each day. I can now look for the beauty in life and see God there. I started this little piece to share about the all-out love I feel for Lilia, my granddaughter. Emily, Matthew and Lilia were just here for about three weeks. I miss them all. I feel joy just thinking about Lilia. I look at pictures of her often throughout the day. I especially like the ones where Elise is feeding her. Life keeps going. Adding Lilia to the loves in my life has not diminished my love for Joy, Elise, Emily, Daniel or the rest of my family. My friend's mother from high school was right, love multiplies. I know the experience of loving and being loved on a daily basis. I know today that my ability to love others is related to my love of God, God's love for me and my ongoing capacity to feel all my emotions.

January 18, 2013   by Joy Pentz.   Marty and I are in the MRI waiting room while Elise gets her routine every two months MRI. She is doing well, so there is probably nothing to worry about. Somehow that does not stop the worrying. The pre MRI worry starts a week or so beforehand. Prayer and acknowledging the fear helps. Elise went back to St Monica to thank them for their prayers and tell about her healing. She did this at their Spanish mass, and spoke in Spanish. I was so proud of her. Sue from work invited Elise to the healing opportunities. Her parents are the leaders of this ministry. Sue's mom Teresa, has been praying for Elise every day at 3:00, and started this months before she ever met Elise. Sunday Elise is going to Nelson's church to do the same thing. Nelson is also from work, and has been praying ceaselessly for Elise. This will be a piece of cake since it's in English. When Elise was on life support and unresponsive, she responded to the voices of Nelson and Byron, also from work. They both have great booming voices, and it gave us hope to see her startle a bit when they said her name. Elise was an intern at my office in. 2010, so she already knew my coworkers, and they have been a great support to all of us. Elise has been coming to my office after class the last two weeks, and everyone is so glad to see her doing so well.

Elise is taking Microeconomics, and took her first quiz yesterday. She thinks she did well. She has been taking driving lessons, but we may end up postponing them because she is afraid to drive and it fatigues her. She asked if she could just take one class next semester also. We told her that the only job she has right now is to get well. We don't expect her to do anything else, but she needs to have some meaningful activity for her spirits. Everyone is amazed when she tells them she is taking Microeconomics, but she chose it because of the Prof. He made economy 101 interesting to her, and she did well. She thought she would have a good chance to be successful at it and then build on that success. She is the one who wanted to go back to school.

The MRI is done. We should know soon. I will update you. Thanks again for everything.

January 18, 2013 by Joy Pentz: YES!!! The tumor is a bit smaller and still low profusion, which means no extra blood vessels to feed any cancer cells. Thank God!

January 19, 2013 by Marty Pentz, 2134 hours. Happy birthday Tommy. I got sober in my mid 20's and thankfully did not know how much I did not know. As I have shared in previous writings, I was closed off emotionally. I did not think I was a fearful person. Turns out I was afraid of just about everything worthwhile in life and did not know it. It was not until my first marriage was crumbling around me that I began to get a hint of my fear of intimacy. Fear is defined as perceiving something as a threat in some fashion. I saw letting people know me as a threat when the real threat was not letting anybody in. I have often heard the phrase "fear of God." I often let that keep me from actively seeking God. I now know that can mean reverence or awe of God. Awe is what I often experience in life today.

2134 hours the 15th of January 2013. I feel less fear tonight. I shared a lot of my life and sober experience tonight. I felt good doing it even though I was quite scattered. When we come up to each MRI we all experience more anxiety and fear. Even while working I spend much of my time praying. I have been praying for so many years that I seem to be saying a prayer in the back of my mind when I am otherwise occupied. This is an amazing blessing of having been pushed and then deciding to continue all the internal work that I do for all these years. I don't see this as some great virtue of mine, but a necessity to stay even close to sane and content with life. With all the pain and suffering there is still much joy in my life. I have learned that in order to feel the joy and contentment I need to be willing to feel the strong negative emotions of fear, sadness, etc. as well.

2101 the 19th of January 2013. The MRI on Friday showed that Elise's tumor was just a smidge smaller than it was two months ago. There is also little or no profusion, blood supply, to the tumor. The tumor cannot live without blood. Her clinical presentation is getting better all the time as well. She has more energy, is thinking better and is doing well in school. I am blessed. I heard a speaker tonight share her recovery story and she was inspiring. I was thinking as she shared how grateful I am that God put Joy and I in each other's path when we were each ready. I have some peace tonight. Goodnight.

February 17, 2013   by Joy Pentz: Hi All. Just a note to let you know Elise is doing well. She has regained some of her energy, facial expressions and intonation. She is using her Thera-putty and exercising everyday so she does not lose what she gained in rehab. She is doing better than expected. It is amazing how little damage was done by such a big tumor in the thalamus. Thanks for all your prayers and support. Joy

March 14, 2013   by Marty Pentz, 2227 hours. Fear can be such an ephemeral thing. It only lasts if I let it hang around and decrease the joy in my life. Letting go and letting God is such a simple thing to say and sometimes so difficult to accomplish. I do this the most effectively when I am praying, meditating, and singing daily and talking to others in recovery every day. Elise is doing well. She did not pass her driving test yesterday and can retake it in six months. Her spatial judgment is still off and almost hit a car; the instructor had to apply the brake. I feel blessed that she did this during the test and not on her own after passing and hit something. She is ok with this now. Tomorrow is her next MRI, hence the fear discussed above. I am comforted by believing that God has her and loves her more than I do. Joy has no fear about tomorrow, she told me she has no doubts the tumor will be smaller again tomorrow. I am 90 some percent there. Talking with Joy tonight and this writing is comforting me and knowing that all my friends that will read this will be praying and/or thinking of Elise, Joy and me. I miss Daniel, getting to know Sara (Daniel's fiancée) Emily, Lilia, and Matthew. I also find it comforting that they are out in the world building their own lives with those they love. "We can easily forgive a child who is afraid of the dark; the real tragedy of life is when men are afraid of the Light." Plato.

March 15, 2013 by Joy Pentz: Elise's tumor is stable, a tiny bit smaller. No report on the profusion yet, but the doctor is not worried about that because the tumor has not grown so it should not have developed additional blood vessels. This is the first time I was not terrified about the MRI. I have no idea why. Elise and I drove to Tulsa last week to visit my parents, sisters and nieces. Dad is doing such a remarkable job being Mom's caregiver. She is bedridden and just started on home hospice care. She didn't seem to know who we were, but she knew she has a daughter named Joy. She still has her sense of humor. When we told her she has been married to Dad for 60 years, she said, "Poor man!"

Mom has to be repositioned every two hours, and it is painful for her. She has always been so sweet and docile, it is amazing to see her aggressive protests when she knows it's coming. She keeps saying she doesn't know how she is going to get out of there when she gets comfortable again. It was hard seeing her like this, but she has been declining for at least 7 years, and watching that decline was even more difficult. Elise really enjoyed spending time with her cousins, and it was great to see my nieces. Everyone was amazed at how well Elise is doing. She still has a somewhat flat affect, but Carol said it's much better than when she saw her in January. I feel like I have PTSD from watching Elise decline, mentally and physically, steadily each day before she was hospitalized. I have flashbacks to those memories and feelings. Watching a funny show helps. Thank goodness for DVR and Big Bang Theory!

March 16, 2013 by Marty Pentz, 1829 hours. Elise's MRI showed that the tumor is a little smaller than two months ago. God is good. The Trinity Episcopal Church, Indianapolis, of which I am a part, is singing the 13th century hymn Stabat Mater tomorrow at 3pm. There is very little I love doing more than singing this very old sacred music we often sing. I experience the Joy of God in this music as much as I do in the love in my life. In a meeting of the fellowship I belong to last night we discussed fear as it related to changes in life like job loss and other issues. I might have been a little over the top in my expression of disdain for the statement in one of our books that talks about acceptance being the answer to all of my problems and that absolutely nothing happens in God's world by mistake. Cancer, child abuse and all the other evils in this world do not come from a loving God, they are mistakes of humanity. There is a prayer that explains better than I can how I see this. "Lord, we pray not for tranquility, nor that our tribulations may cease; we pray for thy spirit and love, that thou grant us strength and grace to overcome adversity; . . . Amen. -- Girolamo Savonarola, 15th Century

April 3, 2013 by Marty Pentz, 2217 hours. This has been a glorious day. For the first time since sometime around Christmas of 2011 Elise sang through a whole choir rehearsal. She was heartily welcomed back. This is the choir that came to the hospital and sang to her and to us while she was semi-comatose in May of last year. I started singing in this choir because Elise was there and I have been so richly blessed by what we sing. I did not know I loved these quite old sacred Anglican Hymns so much. I do not know what or when I wrote last, but her tumor is smaller still at her last MRI. This phase of treatment is scheduled to end near the end of June and we are unsure how we are going to proceed from there. She said the other day how much she loves her life.   I am now ready to proceed with the writing of this story or memoir to whatever date the Spirit moves me to write to and from. When I looked back over some of my earlier writing I realized my reluctance was due to not being ready to look at those days prior to Elise being near death and the time in intensive care. I can look at that time now without wanting to cry a lot. I will be posting more often for a time. We Skype with Lilia, Emily and Matthew almost every Saturday now and that has been a great way to keep in touch. Received a text from Daniel the other day and Sara and he are planning their wedding. Life is moving forward and God is good. "Music is an agreeable harmony for the honor of God and the permissible delights of the soul. Johann Sebastian Bach. "If music be the food of love, play on." William Shakespeare. "After silence, that which comes nearest to expressing the inexpressible is music." Aldous Huxley.

April 23, 2013. This is Elise! I'm volunteering at Riley and am very very bored but grateful I'm even able to be here. I was just reading the guestbook and realized I should give the people what they want, an update. I dropped out of school because I was a bit over-confident in my learning abilities and apparently microeconomics is a hard class for people without brain tumors so I had to drop it. I decided, after hearing an inspiring sermon at church on Easter, to switch majors to Visual Communications and get an AAS at Ivy Tech and I'll start going in the fall. I'm excited! I also decided to rejoin the church choir, which is hard but very enriching and fulfilling and FUN! Plus it's great to share the experience with my wonderful dad. I hear that exercise can help brain tumors so I'm trying to get at least 30 minutes of exercise a day (not to mention Abilify made me gain about 15 unwanted pounds).

May 10, 2013 by Joy Pentz: Elise had an MRI today, and the tumor is stable and still appears to be dead!!! She also got her PICC line out today. She probably broke a record being able to maintain it for 10 months, and it was still fine. She was going to get it taken out early for camp anyway, and she was tired of having to keep it dry and having the dressing changed each week. Only 3 more Avastin infusions and two more rounds of Temodar! Elise will be going to Camp Make a Dream in Montana next month for a Heads Up Conference with other brain tumor patients age 18-25. She will get to see the Minnesota part of the family on the way there. Later in August she will go west again to Daniel and Sara's wedding in CA.

Elise has returned to choir as an alto. She didn't go back sooner because she couldn't reach all the high notes, and she wanted to remain a soprano. Her vocal cords have not recovered fully from the trach yet. She calls her trach scar her battle scar, and does not try to cover it up. The choir had a Cabaret fundraiser, and she sang and danced as one of the Downtown Ladies in the song Downtown by Petula Clark. And to think that this time about a year ago she was on life support, and not expected to live. Members of the choir came to the hospital to sing for her each week, and cheered up the whole neuro ICU.

From Marty May 13, 2013 2140 hours. The MRI last Friday showed Elise's tumor was stable, as we want and they took her PICC line out. She is doing very well and is surviving and thriving beyond all expectations, except for God's. What an amazing blessing. We see Emily, Lilia and Matthew about once per week on Skype. Daniel is getting married in August. Many blessings in our life. This quote is how I often feel. "The unthankful heart discovers no mercies; but the thankful heart will find, in every hour, some heavenly blessings." Henry Ward Beecher.

June 20, 2013 by Joy Pentz: Elise was in Montana last week for Heads Up conference/camp for brain cancer survivors. She found out about it online and was excited about going. When she first arrived she sent a text saying how grateful she was she didn't have the kind of deficits she saw in the other people. She said she felt like she was one of the only normal people there. All the people there were age 18-25, but most had been diagnosed before age 10, and were not able to develop normally and seemed stuck in childhood. Many had speech and language problems as well as cognitive and vision deficits. She felt like she didn't fit in, but did not want to fit in. She felt bad about herself for being judgmental. She felt trapped and homesick, and wanted to come home because being there made her feel like she was mentally retarded (her words)

I spoke with her therapist who theorized that most of the time she could live her life without dwelling on the fact that she has a brain tumor, but seeing 64 people with the same condition who seemed so abnormal put her predicament in her face. Since she returned I feel overwhelmed by the miracle that she is alive and doing so well. I also feel overwhelmed by the miracle of the Internet which led us to minimally invasive laser surgery for her "inoperable" tumor and information about alternative/integrative remedies others have used to strengthen the immune system and kill cancer cells before they develop into tumors. Through the Internet and cancer forums we have been encouraged by stories of long term survivors whose doctors "gave" them months to live.

July 25, 2013   by Joy Pentz: Elise had her first post chemo MRI and her tumor is still stable with no blood supply. I have not been scared of hearing MRI results since we have had a series of good ones and Elise is getting to be more and more like her old self. But... as we were waiting for the results Dr. Jessica was examining Elise, and for the first time she answered yes to questions about headaches and blurry vision and I was shocked because she never said anything about it to us. Then when she was holding her arms out straight to see if her left arm drifted down, Dr. Jessica kept looking at her for a long time so I thought maybe she was drifting. Dr. Jessica then said, "Let me have someone read the MRI." When she came back and said it was stable I was so relieved. She said she noticed I was about to jump out of my chair when Elise said yes to headaches and blurry vision. Dr. Jessica's husband is a radiologist so she can sometimes get results very quickly.

We are changing some of Elise's meds post chemo, so that could have been the reason for her symptoms. If I ever doubted depression was a physical, chemical phenomenon, I don't anymore. Elise had gradually gotten more depressed since she stopped Abilify. I asked if she could try Wellbutrin instead of Cymbalta. After a week on only 75 mg added to her Cymbalta, she was feeling much better and stopped having thoughts of wishing she didn't have to live anymore, which she could not get through a day without. She was scheduled to take 150. Mg after a week. Within a few days of the increased dose, she became suicidal to the point of waking me up (thank God) in the middle of the night to tell me she woke up thinking of taking a cab to Oaklandon and laying down on the train tracks. She had also looked on the Internet for ways to be successful, but as she pointed out, there are very few first-hand accounts from those who were successful at suicide.

> *Comment by Joy, January 15, 2018. Less than a month prior to Elise's tumor diagnosis, unbeknownst to us, she drove herself to a nearby branch of an outpatient clinic, and asked the receptionist what she should do if she wants to drive her car off a bridge. The receptionist told her to drive to their hospital for inpatient care. The hospital was about 20 miles away, with more than one bridge. Fortunately Elise got there safely, and was admitted as an inpatient. She stayed about a week, but during that time she slept through many of the group therapy sessions. After she was released with antidepressants, she continued to get worse, and had to withdraw from her college classes. We set up a sleep study for her, and I remember when we told her about it, she barely registered what we said, and looked at us with glassy eyes and no expression on her face. I had to look away, it was so disturbing. She told us later that she had been feeling the compulsion to drive off a bridge for a while. Research shows that brain injury increases the risk of suicide, and that this may explain why so many veterans with TBI (traumatic brain injury) from IEDs (improvised explosive devices) commit suicide. (Fisher, L. B., Pedrelli, P., Iverson, G. L., Bergquist, T. F., Bombardier, C. H., Hammond, F. M., ... Zafonte, R. (2016). Prevalence of suicidal behaviour following traumatic brain injury: Longitudinal follow-up data from the NIDRR Traumatic Brain Injury Model Systems. Brain Injury, 1-8. DOI: 10.1080/02699052.2016.1195517)*

I didn't let her out of my sight and cut her dose per the doctor back to 75 mg. Within a few days she was back to no more thoughts of death, and after a week she feels wonderful. The fact that she woke me up and was willing to sleep in bed with me with an alarmed door and let me follow her around shows she really wants to live. Right before she was diagnosed with the brain tumor, she became suicidal and that is not surprising based on the location that regulates mood. The other med we are changing is going from Keppra to Vimpat to prevent seizures. It is unclear from her 24 hour EEG and video whether changes in her brain activity showed a seizure. Since seizures are so common with brain tumors the neurologist advised to stay on anticonvulsants, but hopes the change will help her fatigue and mood. So far, so good, and she is still in the process of weaning off Keppra.

Yesterday Elise texted me that she felt wonderful. That's the first time she used that word since this all began. What a journey this is. How precious life is. How important good spirits are. I can see the light at the end of the tunnel now that Elise has enough energy not to spend most of her time sleeping....which brings me to today's big event.

We have an appointment finally to go over Elise's neuropsychological assessment and her interests and abilities assessment with her voc rehab counselor. He has been so slow to do his part every step along the way. He has had the report from the psychologist for weeks, but would not return my calls to set up an appointment so Elise can get going for the fall semester. Finally, I asked Marty to call, thinking he might be more responsive to a man. Sure enough he returned the call the same morning, and made an appointment for the same week. Thank you for all your interest, support and prayers. I seriously could not be getting through this without you.

> *Comment by Marty, February 3, 2018: Elise survives brain cancer, and then her depression gets so deep, she tries to kill herself by driving off a bridge. The day this happened, Joy and I got home from work, and she was nowhere to be found. There were some very intense hours until we found out she was safe in the psychiatric ward. Depression can be insidious and very scary. When I was about four years into recovery, I woke up emotionally. I did not wake up pretty. I became suicidal, and was not safe to be alone. My sponsor let me sleep on his couch for three weeks until I was safe. Sometime prior to waking up emotionally, I did not think I had the emotion of love, that I was dead to the world emotionally.*

> *Over time, the diseases of addiction and depression can cause one to think there are only two choices, using again or death. Recovery begins when we can see a glimpse of hope for a different life. Add in brain cancer/tumor, and life becomes quite the challenge.*

> *"Some days 24 hours is too much to stay put in, so I take the day hour by hour, moment by moment. I break the task, the challenge, the fear into small, bite-size pieces. I can handle a piece of fear,*

depression, anger, pain, sadness, loneliness, illness. I actually put my hands up to my face, one next to each eye, like blinders on a horse" Regina Brett

I feel blessed to be able to feel all of this experience with Elise, as much as it can hurt. The long journey moves forward.

I wrote the above when Elise was reading a story to Joy while Joy was cooking. The blessings of "normal" life.

August 17, 2013 by Joy Pentz: We are in California for Sara and Daniel's wedding. Elise was marveling at the views from the airplane. She feels like she just woke up a few weeks ago, and is so happy to be alive. Her antidepressant and anti-seizure meds have been tweaked, and she feels so much better. She has more energy, her face isn't sweating all the time, her skin isn't itchy, and she no longer feels depressed. She also started on Buspar for her anxiety and restlessness. She is much calmer, and her bouncing, knuckle cracking and hair pulling have diminished. She no longer has a flat affect, and her sense of humor is back. She has had short periods of nausea, headache and blurry vision which coincided with starting the therapeutic dose of Vimpat and starting Buspar, but those symptoms are subsiding. We were a bit panicky because those are the symptoms she had with the growth of her tumor. We felt relieved when we looked at the side effects of her meds. We are learning to appreciate the present moment without worrying about the future.

SARA AND DANIEL'S WEDDING, AUGUST 19, 2013

ELISE AT SARA AND DANIEL'S WEDDING---HAIR GROWING BACK, SMILE
LESS CROOKED, FACE LESS STIFF

MRI stable!   by Joy Pentz, October 25, 2013   Elise had an MRI today, and there were no changes. The tumor is still dead, and all her labs are normal. Thank God! She occasionally has mild headaches and nausea, and it's hard not to worry about a recurrence. We are both exhausted from our trip to England to visit Emily, Matthew and Lilia. We had a great time. Tonight we went to Drew's sister's wedding, and it was so wonderful to see Elise dancing. Thank you for your continued prayers.

Elise just passed her driving test!!!! By Joy Pentz, November 5, 2013: No highway driving quite yet, though.

November 22, 2013 by Joy Pentz: I was looking at the Cleveland Clinic website because I had responded to a forum discussion of the American Brain Tumor Association about Elise's surgery there. Someone had written that her tumor was inoperable because it is in her thalamus like Elise's. The AutoLitt surgery equipment is in its second generation now, and it is called NeuroBlate. Cleveland Clinic added an illustrated brochure about it, and there were pictures of a doctor looking at MRI images showing a tumor that looked like Elise's and drawings illustrating the procedure using the example of a tumor in the right thalamus. When Gail, the nurse from there, called to tell me that Dr Barnett agrees with Elise's MRI report and is thrilled, I asked her about the brochure. Sure enough, I did recognize Elise's tumor. I told Gail if they ever want to use her face or a video I'm sure Elise would love that. She said she would let their marketing department know. They recently showed a video of a patient on CBN and received a hundred calls.

When I told Elise about it she said she always wanted to be famous. Actually, she was in a couple of commercials when she was little. She was one of the kids who won a lip sync contest for a radio station to be in a TV commercial. They dressed a second grader Elise up in a leopard outfit with a feathered boa around her neck and glamorous hair and makeup. They had her bat her eyelashes and throw the boa over her shoulder while she did a lip sync to Shania Twain's song "Man, I Feel Like a Woman". It was so adorable, a radio station in Oregon bought her footage for their commercial and paid her $500 for it. The kids in the Indy commercial were on the news showing them getting out of a limo and going into the Hard Rock Cafe to see a premier of the commercial and be presented with the $100 they won.

When she was in preschool, Elise played Darla from Spanky and our Gang in a commercial for the Sunshine Cafe. She was supposed to be pulled in a wagon, and she even had a line. She did fine in rehearsal, but got shy during the shoot. They used footage of her at the end running up on stage frantically looking for the parting in the stage curtain so she could go backstage. She was such an adorable kid with her Shirley Temple hair and her freckles. Now she is a beautiful woman with her Betty Boop hair and her freckles. I guess she got a taste of being famous and liking it. She is looking forward to the possibility of sharing her surgical miracle for the non-profit Cleveland Clinic. I'll suggest that they can show how they were able to preserve her speech and language ability and her ear for music by having her sing about her medical adventure. Not exactly what she had in mind when she dreamed of fame, but still....

Renewed prayer by Joy Pentz. November 28, 2013. Please renew your prayers and prayer networks for Elise. She is in the Crisis Behavioral Unit at Community North Hospital after attempting suicide in the car. She is physically ok. She has given us permission to write about this here, but not on Facebook (she does have some common sense). We are so grateful she did not succeed, but so scared that she tried. We had no idea where she was. She was brought to the ER by police and then to the psych unit for a 24 hour hold. We decided to call hospitals when she did not show up at her NA meeting, and we learned she had been treated and released from the ER. They could not tell us anything else because she is not a minor. One kind person gave us a phone number to call, without telling us directly that she was there.

Finally after many hours she filled out a form listing who the hospital could give info to, and we spoke with the person who did the assessment and then we were able to speak with Elise. They only have short visiting hours Wed and Sun, but special times for Thanksgiving. She agreed to stay past the 24 hour hold as a voluntary patient. Otherwise they would have had to go to court to get a 72 hour hold. Elise has not seemed depressed lately, and if she was, she was not aware of it. She has had lots of anxiety about becoming independent. She is uncertain about her ability to ever earn a living, and is anxious about feeling so dependent on us financially and emotionally. I think we are saying all the right things to encourage her while at the same time assuring her that she is always welcome to depend on us as long as necessary.

Sometimes Elise's thoughts and fears send her into a tailspin of panic. The panic, along with the poor impulse control, often caused by brain injuries, makes her want to take her life to make the panic attack stop. I have heard that panic attacks can make you feel like you are dying. She has always told someone when she feels that way, but this time she felt if she didn't do it right then, she would never do it, and she would regret it the next time she had another panic attack. It has only been the last month or so that she has become alert and awake enough to understand the gravity of her diagnosis and how close to death she was. She has thanked us repeatedly for not listening to the doctors who wanted to pull the plug when she was on life support, and adores the one doctor who had just enough hope to give her a chance; she told us Elise's chances were not 0%.

Elise did not notice anyone behind her when she attempted to drive off a bridge, but there was a firefighter, and he stayed with her until the police came. She was not able to deny it was a suicide attempt because the firefighter told police she made a sudden deliberate left turn into the retaining wall. She bounced backwards, hitting the other retaining wall and spinning around. There was no oncoming traffic. She had her seatbelt on and the airbag deployed. It was surprising even to her that she had her seatbelt on, but it's a good habit, and when she started off her only intent was to drive home. Needless to say, she has lost her driving privileges, and the car is not drivable. One of the police officers who was guarding her at the hospital was someone she went to summer camp with in middle school, and had an internet relationship with afterwards. He did not remember her because he had also had a head injury!

I am feeling amazingly calm, in large part due to what I have learned in my support group for family and friends of alcoholics/addicts. Also, I am so relieved after hours of having a missing child. She always answers our texts, but her phone was confiscated. I am also relieved she is in a safe place for now, and she is attending group therapy and learning how to deal with panic attacks. Thanks for all your love, support and prayers.

December 1, 2013   by Joy Pentz. Not really much to update, but...Elise will probably come home today or tomorrow. They don't keep patients long these days. She has learned a lot from the many groups she has attended. They raised her Buspar dosage for anxiety, and she said it has really helped. The doctors think her depression is under control, which is really a relief. With depression, her thoughts of not wanting to live are pretty constant. With anxiety, these thoughts only come when she lets the anxiety escalate to panic. She is learning how to incorporate daily activities that prevent anxiety and measures to stop the escalation to panic if she becomes anxious.

Marty and I are really scared about keeping her safe, but we decided to focus on this being a new beginning for Elise's healing. She has agreed to go to group therapy and she has promised to call someone if she feels suicidal. Of course, she had made that promise in the past and only broke it this one time.... :) Someone described the ups and downs when his daughter had similar issues as feeling like you are on the end of a whip. Great analogy. We are trying to get off the whip by living in the moment as much as possible. Marty went to a retreat recently, and the leader gave them a card that says, "Left, Right, Breathe, Turn it Over." We are making that our mantra---just take the next step, breathe to stay calm, and turn our worries over to God to give us strength and hope and to take care of his child, Elise. Sometimes I picture myself turning Elise over and rolling her off a cliff, trusting that God will catch her, and that picture helps me. It also helps to remember the 3 Cs. I didn't cause it, I can't cure it and I can't control it.

> *Comment by Marty, February 4, 2018: Panic can be paralyzing or create the felt need to do something irrational to stop the panic. Blessedly, between her meds and learned skills, Elise has been able to lessen anxiety before it goes to panic.*

December 29, 2013 by Joy Pentz: It's been awhile since I updated you. Elise is grateful her suicide attempt failed. She frequently thanks us for not pulling the plug when she needed the ventilator. She started going to St. Vincent Stress Center intensive outpatient group therapy for young adults 3X/ week for 3 hours per day. It has been good for her and for us. We join them for family group sessions an hour per week. The doubling of her dose of Buspar for anxiety seems to be helping her as well.

Elise's suicide attempt has shaken us up, especially Marty, who deals with veterans with PTSD who are suicidal and sometimes succeed in their attempts. A month before Elise's tumor diagnosis, she checked herself into the stress center because she was feeling suicidal, so she has come full circle. The damage caused by the tumor affects her impulse control, depression and anxiety. Elise decided to postpone trying to take another class, which is wise. She is still too fatigued to add this to her schedule, and it will postpone her being around tall buildings downtown. She had contemplated jumping off one when she felt panic, and there are no second chances with that. Thanks to my sister Doreen's suggestion, we now have a dog, Lucy, we hope to train to be a service dog to alert Elise to her anxiety to prevent full blown panic attacks.

Elise was very excited about getting a dog, but we are a bit disappointed in her level of attention to Lucy so far. It's only been a few weeks, so hopefully that will improve. Lucy is Marty's first dog, and we are both loving having her in our lives. She is calm, obedient, smart and so affectionate. We start formal obedience training Jan 7. Lucy is a 2 year old rescue dog who was thought to be a Labradoodle, but when we took her to the vet, he thought she was a Terrier mix based on her lack of shedding. There is less hair left in her brush than in mine after brushing. Whatever she is she seems perfect for us. Thank you for continuing to keep Elise in your prayers.

> *Comment by Joy, January 4, 2018. At some point we got tired of not knowing the answer when people asked us what breed Lucy is, so she had a DNA test to find out. She is Afghan, Chow Chow, Corgi and Dobermann Pinscher. It's quite interesting to think her ancestors came from Afghanistan, China, Wales and Germany. We all love her, but Marty is crazy about her. She has been very healing for us.*

> *Comment by Marty, February 4, 2018: I do not recall ever wanting a dog, but Lucy has been an amazing blessing from God. I was having frequent nightmares involving Elise and brain cancer. Almost immediately after getting Lucy, they stopped. I did not know I needed a dog. Elise came across a bumper sticker with a picture of a dog that said, "Who rescued whom?"*

ELISE AND OUR RESCUE DOG, LUCY - AN AFGHAN, CHOW CHOW, CORGI, AND DOBERMANN MIX, ACCORDING TO A DNA TEST.

January 18, 2014, by Joy Pentz.   Another stable MRI, thank God.

March 15, 2014 by Joy Pentz. Just an update...You would not believe how well Elise is doing. Her survival is a miracle, but just as miraculous is her lack of physical or cognitive deficits. It is very common for people with head trauma and brain injuries, whether from accidents, tumors or stroke, to develop a seizure disorder, which she has not. Others are left with speech and language problems, and she is unscathed in that area. She completes a crossword puzzle daily, and is starting to do the word jumble as well. It is very common to have physical problems such as paralysis, tremors and/or weakness. Elise's left hand is not as strong as her right, but she purposely uses her left hand instead of her dominant hand to do things, and she faithfully uses her strengthening putty to improve. The therapy putty is like silly putty. We embedded it with little beads which she has to find and remove with her left hand. She does this while riding a stationary bike for exercise each day. She will probably never become ambidextrous, but who among us ever does? We are most grateful that our smart, witty, personable, bubbly daughter is back, and her flat affect is gone. We can live with the fact that she still has a bit of a crooked smile. Elise's voice has strengthened to the point that she has performed solos and duets (with me no less). No plans of "giving up our day jobs"' to become the Pentz's, largely because the Pentz's doesn't roll off the tongue like the Judd's for example. Help us find a good name for our duo, and who knows?

Speaking of voices, she and I are going to become voice donors. I learned about this opportunity from the Ted Talk Radio Hour podcast called Extrasensory. Did you know that all people who use speech synthesizing devises sound the same as Stephen Hawking regardless of gender or age? A speech scientist has found a way to use whatever sounds a person can make and blend it with the speech donor's voice to custom make a synthesizer so the person sounds like themselves. The donor records a three hour reading, and all the sounds of the language become available for the person to utter any syllables, words and sentences they want.

They interviewed an 11 year old girl with cerebral palsy and her mom. The girl did not sound like a computer voice, and the mom is so grateful to be able to have conversations with her daughter after 11 years. Her daughter is so chatty now, the mom jokes that at times she has thoughts of turning off her synthesizer.

I love listening to podcasts like Ted Talks, Radiolab and Healing Cancer Gently. They always lift my spirit and give me hope for humanity. I have learned from podcasts, books and internet research that there are over 300 known foods, plants, herbs and other remedies that have been used for millennia by humans to prevent and heal cancer with success. Many meds are derived from plants, so this is not surprising. We are throwing the kitchen sink at Elise to provide the right environment for her immune system to take care of all the cancer cells we all regularly develop. We are grateful she cooperates with us. Of course these remedies will never be proven with double blind studies because they cannot be patented, and it takes millions of dollars to do the studies required for FDA approval. It is enough for me to know we are giving Elise things which will not hurt her, and which are being used by long term cancer survivors.

Good news/bad news, by Joy Pentz.   April 25, 2014. Elise had her quarterly MRI today, and Peyton Manning was visiting his namesake children's hospital, and took a picture with her. Elise's MRI showed the solid part of her tumor is still stable, but the cystic part of the tumor has grown. The blood profusion is fine on all parts of the tumor, which means it is probably dead. We have appointments Mon and Tues with the radiation oncologist and neurosurgeon. Also the MRI is being overnighted to Elise's neurosurgeon at Cleveland Clinic. Elise will probably have surgery to drain the fluid of the cyst and test it, and possibly a biopsy of the solid part. Please keep her in your thoughts and prayers. .

Marty Pentz April 27, 2014 · 2308 hours the 26th of April 2014: We are embarking on another adventure with Elise and her tumor. The MRI on Friday showed a cyst on the outside of the solid tumor. It is unknown at this time if it is simply benign or more cancer. We will see the neurosurgeon Tuesday that did a couple of her procedures in Indianapolis and hopefully have a phone consult on Monday with the surgeon at the Cleveland Clinic that did her laser ablation procedure. There is no profusion (blood supply) to the solid tumor or the cyst, which is a good sign. Our spirits are mostly good as this point and simply loving each day together. Our faith and trust in God and the surgeons is strong. I am not sleeping well, but doing fundamentally well. I am watching the Minnesota hockey game while I type this. Elise is neurologically sound, which is also a good sign. Please keep praying. "Never be afraid to trust an unknown future to a known God." — Corrie ten Boom

Action plan, by Joy Pentz, May 3, 2014.   All of the doctors who have viewed Elise's MRI so far agree on the MRI interpretation and action plan. Her MRI will also be presented at the next tumor board where neurosurgeons and neurooncologists meet to confer with each other about tumors. Everyone so far agrees that the cystic looking part looks to be a fluid filled cyst, and not viable tumor, but you cannot always tell from an MRI. The Cleveland Clinic surgeon said he would be able to Neuro-Blate it if necessary. Neuro-Blate is the new and improved version of the AutoLitt laser ablation surgery Elise had in Feb of 2012. That is a relief.   No one knows why some tumors form benign cysts. The solid part of Elise's dead looking (based on lack of abnormal blood flow) tumor will be biopsied, and the cyst will be drained with a big enough hole to prevent it from growing back together and filling up again. All agree that the cyst would continue to grow and eventually cause neurological symptoms.

Endoscopic stereotactic surgery is scheduled for May 14 at St Vincent Hospital in Indy. This will be Elise's fifth brain surgery since this "adventure" began in Dec of 2011.   The good news is that this has made Elise realize she really wants to live. She said if this thing is going to kill her she is not going to go down without fighting for her life. She said she doesn't want to be anyone's cancer story to tell of the girl with brain cancer who gave up or killed herself. This determination has invigorated her, and has all but eliminated her anxiety and depression.

I feel as if all the hope-filled pockets of anxiety I have been carrying around all these months have been pierced and have filled my body with exhaustion. I am trying to let go of what I cannot control and concentrate on savoring each moment of life. My natural reaction is to be alone so I can concentrate on distracting myself from my fears, but it doesn't make any sense to miss out on any time I could be spending with the person I fear losing. I don't know what I would do without all of your support, thoughts and prayers. Please continue. It helps to be greeted each day by our new dog Lucy who can hardly contain herself, she is always so happy to see us.

May 7, 2014, by Joy Pentz: Thank you for all you thoughts, prayers and support. I am comforted by your messages and "likes" on Caringbridge as well as your in-person support. I read the Caringbridge guest book frequently for encouragement, especially when I wake up in the middle of the night, which is often these days, so please don't hesitate to write a quick message. I am having a difficult time not projecting into the future and thinking about and reliving the dread of two years ago when Elise was in ICU and not expected to live.

Yesterday Elise drove by herself a short distance for the first time since her "incident" in Nov. She has been driving with Marty in the car. She said her thoughts as she drove were, "I love my life" and how different those thoughts were from the last time she drove by herself. I ask her to rate her depression and anxiety every day from 1 to 10, and the ratings are low or zero. It is amazing what medications can do. I know her therapy and the support help a lot, but increasing her Buspar and Wellbutrin made such a difference almost immediately.   Yesterday Elise told me one of the young men she met at "brain tumor camp" last summer died. She said he was one of the only ones who seemed normal. It made both of us sad and scared. Please keep your thoughts, prayers and messages of support coming. Thanks, Joy

Surgery day today, by Joy Pentz, May 14, 2014:   Elise was just taken to MRI for her pre-surgery scan. Dr Y will use it to plan the path in her brain to her cyst and tumor. It is endoscopic surgery, so they just drill a small hole. Marty and I both had trouble sleeping last night. This is the first surgery where Elise is well enough to make the decision and give her consent. The nurses are so sweet at St Vincent. She asked them if being pretty is a requirement here. She needed a second nurse to help with the IV because her veins are so small. I have the same problem, and in fact was told to stop trying to donate blood because my veins collapse.

Elise did her daily crossword puzzle in the waiting room. I told her how grateful I am that she is still so smart when she instantly got the answer "filament" for thread. She said let's hope I'm still smart after surgery. Yesterday she and I beaded a necklace, and she was easily able to string the very small beads. At one point she would not have been able to do that because of double vision and lack of strength and coordination. I need to remind myself of the miracle of her life when I am fearful.   Thank you for all your messages, texts and emails, and especially your thoughts, prayers and encouragement. I will send another message after her surgery.

Unbelievable! No surgery today, by Joy Pentz, May 14, 2014:   The MRI showed the cyst was one fourth the size, and the solid part of the tumor is the same!

Marty Pentz May 14, 2014 · 1623 hours. "The Age of Miracles is still with us." Elise was to have her fifth brain surgery today. When Dr. Y saw the pre-op MRI it was only a ¼ the size it was last month, no surgery needed at this time. The cyst is shrinking. Please keep praying. I do not ride roller coasters anymore as they make me ill. I have been living on one heck of an emotional roller coaster since the 10th of December 2011 when we found the tumor. Elise had gone back for the surgery and Drew and I went down for lunch. They give you this pager so they can find you when the surgery is complete and the doctor wants to talk with you. I had taken one bite of food when the pager went off and my initial reaction was "what the f…" The only thing I could think of was that she had a reaction to the anesthesia. Going up the stairs I met Dr. Y coming down looking for us. He stated that when he looked at the MRI it was dramatically different than the last one and we needed to talk about it. I quickly asked him if it was a good thing and he said yes.

We went and rounded up Joy and Drew and that is when he told us the cyst was so much smaller and he did not see a need for surgery. My emotions at first were weirdly silent. I had been prepared emotionally for the weight of surgery and then the news it was not necessary left me almost speechless. Speechless is not my normal state. Right now I am calm and elated at the same time. What a strange combination of emotions. God is good and we keep praying. "There is in every child at every stage a new miracle of vigorous unfolding, which constitutes a new hope and a new responsibility for all." Erik Erikson "We are the miracle of force and matter making itself over into imagination and will. Incredible. The Life Force experimenting with forms. You for one. Me for another. The Universe has shouted itself alive. We are one of the shouts." Ray Bradbury.

Great day. By Joy Pentz, June 26, 2014:   Elise and I had a great day today. We went to the 50th year celebration of the passing of the Civil Rights Act of 1964. This law created the EEOC, Equal Employment Opportunity Commission, where I have worked for 22 years. It was an inspiring program, and made me feel proud to be a part of something so big and life changing for our country. The speakers were truly inspiring to me. The other thing that was so wonderful about today was seeing and feeling all the love my coworkers showered down on Elise. She was an intern at the EEOC five years ago, so she already knew my coworkers before her brain cancer was diagnosed. Then when she was so sick they rallied around us and supported us with visits to the hospital, notes on Caringbridge, emails, food, thoughts and prayers. Many of them saw Elise when she was on life support and unresponsive, then learning to walk and talk again. Now she is restored and renewed and transformed by her cancer experience. It was so lovely to share her with my work family today as we celebrated this momentous occasion together.

The celebration took place at a hotel/conference center across the street from the hospital where Elise stayed for seven weeks two years ago. The hospital keeps a room at the hotel for family members of patients to use for an hour and a half. When Elise was in intensive care we slept in the waiting room and alternated sitting with Elise night and day. Each day I would go to the hotel to shower and watch an episode of Law and Order to relax and escape. Today when Elise's fatigue forced her to find a place to lay down, the sweet women at the front desk found her a room to use. What a mixture of bittersweet memories, tragedy and triumph, love and celebration, perspective and gratitude.   ...and then I came home and got to take a walk in the sunshine with the most loving dog in the world. Life is good.

MRI - cyst has disappeared!!!! By Joy Pentz, July 2, 2014.   Elise had an MRI yesterday. The cyst, which had already shrunk considerably, is gone, thank God. The solid part of the dead tumor measured a few mm smaller, but it's hard to tell exact measurements because of its irregular shape and the difficulty of finding the exact same position to measure to compare to the previous MRI. Elise's oncologist expected the cyst to have grown and they would kick themselves for not doing the surgery/biopsy in May. She and the other doctors have no explanation for the disappearance, but we'll take it! All that insomnia was for nothing. I'll try to remember that next time I have something I'm worrying about. Thanks for all your supportive messages, thoughts and prayers.

ELISE AND PEYTON MANNING TAKEN AT PEYTON MANNING CHILDREN'S HOSPITAL

July 23, 2014. Here is something that would not have happened without Elise's cancer "adventure"---meeting and getting her picture taken with Peyton Manning. We happened to be at an appointment with Elise's pediatric neurooncologist at Peyton Manning Children's Hospital. This picture was taken last winter, but it was just sent to us. Elise's face is no longer stiff looking with a flat affect. She is back to her more bubbly self, most of the time, and her face is back to normal except for her adorable crooked smile that remains. Elise has recently added the crypto-quip puzzle to her daily crossword and jumble puzzles from the newspaper. Two years ago she could not remember a series of three words and we had to give her only liquids because she could not remember to chew, and could not eat without choking. I need to find a way to be grateful for how far she has come without reliving the horror of the past and the fear of the future. I thank God for the miracle of her life. Thank you all for your support.

September 10, 2014 by Joy Pentz: Just a note to let you know Elise is still doing well. Her miraculous recovery continues. She seems to have hit a plateau with regaining her energy. She still needs to take one or two naps during the day. We had her set up to have a sleep study right before her tumor diagnosis, but cancelled it when she was diagnosed. We may go ahead and do a sleep study in case that needs to be addressed. Thank you for your support.

MRI day, by Joy Pentz, January 20, 2015. Another good, stable MRI. Yippee!!! Although the radiologist report said the tumor was stable and still dead, both Dr Y, her brain surgeon, and Dr. Jessica, her oncologist, said the tumor is smaller. That means the dead cells are being absorbed by Elise's body. I got the impression for the first time that they both are beginning to think she will make it.

> *Comment by Joy, January 13, 2018: Surprise! A scam or an actual email (see below) from the White House?*
>
> On Feb 3, 2015, at 12:39 PM, "M_____, Caitria" <Caitria_____ @who.eop.gov> wrote:
>
> Joy and Marty –
>
> Hope this email finds you well!

We received your letter to the President would like to invite you and a parent to attend the President's event on Friday at Ivy Tech Community College in Indianapolis, IN.

If you could please send over the following information for you both, I will follow up with the additional information to attend the event.

 Full Name

Date of Birth

Social Security Number

 Thanks, and we hope you can make it!

 All the best,

Caitria

Caitria M_____

Office of Political Strategy & Outreach

The White House

> *Comment by Joy, January 13, 2018: When I saw this email, I almost ignored it because it seemed like it was a scam to get personal identify information. President Obama's visit to Indianapolis had not yet been announced in the news. Just in case it was legitimate, I decided to respond. Here is my response:*

From: Joy Pentz
Sent: Tuesday, February 03, 2015 9:54 PM
To: _____, Caitria
Subject: Re: President Obama in Indiana

 Dear Ms. M_____,

We would love to attend, but are reluctant to give the personal identity information requested without some way to know you are who you say you are. Is there some way for us to verify that this request is legitimate? Thanks, Joy Pentz

> Comment by Joy, January 13, 2018: Instead of an email response, I got a phone call the next day at work from Caitria M_____ of the White House. She said she was calling in response to my email to let me know it was legitimate. She sounded credible, but I am an Investigator, after all, and I need evidence to corroborate what people tell me. I asked her to read the letter I wrote. She had the authentic letter I wrote, so I gave her the information she asked for by phone. Then she hesitantly asked if Elise lived nearby to see if she could make it as well. I think she asked that to avoid asking directly if Elise was still alive. I gave her Elise's information as well. When we actually got there, only Marty and I were on the list. Of course, we were so upset. The person at the desk called someone, and then told us Elise could go in as well.

On Feb 5, 2015 11:55 AM, "M_____, Caitria" <Caitria _____@who.eop.gov> wrote:

Hi Joy – we're happy that you, Marty and Elise will join us tomorrow.

Attached are the instructions for arrival. As stated, doors open at 11:30am, but please do not arrive after 1pm. Let me know if there are any additional questions.

Thanks and enjoy!

Best,

Caitria

Meeting President Obama today! By Joy Pentz, February 6, 2015. President Obama is doing a town hall at Ivy Tech Community College in Indianapolis today. I had written President Obama in 2013, to thank him for Obamacare because it saved Elise's life, so we were invited to sit in the VIP section at the town hall at Ivy Tech today. (Not really sure we will get to meet him, but hoping.) Elise had to drop out of college due to the brain cancer, and since she was 19, she would not have been covered by our insurance had the ACA not extended the age to 26 whether in college or not. Some of the doctors advised us to literally pull the plug, and without insurance... She is now cancer free with no cognitive or physical deficits. The no deficits part is thanks to Dr. B at Cleveland Clinic. She was the 19th patient to have AutoLitt surgery (now called Neuro-Blate), which he helped develop. The surgery cooks the tumor from the inside out with a laser under an intraoperative MRI. Had she had a craniotomy to debulk the tumor, she could have had major deficits because it was so deep in her brain. In fact, we were advised when they thought it was benign, that it was inoperable. You can watch it on WTHR TV in Indianapolis or on live stream on the White House website at 2:00. If someone could record it on DVD, I would appreciate it. Our DVR is set to record it, but I can't transfer it to a DVD. Thank you to all of you for your support and prayers!

We got to thank the President for saving Elise's life! By Joy Pentz, February 6, 2015. We had no idea what would happen today. There were about 40 people on the "clutch" list who were taken to another room who got to shake hands with the President and get our pictures taken with him prior to the town hall. There were three people with family members who were there because we wrote letters to the President, and we got to spend a bit more time with him. Marty and I thanked him for saving Elise's life with the ACA. He told Elise she looked really good, and she said, "Thanks, so do you!" We also got to shake his hand again at the end because we were right up front. We had assigned seats with our names on them. Another letter writer was a single mom, Jillian, who thanked the President for a Pell Grant that is helping her finish her degree to support her children after her husband left. She also thanked him for his Precision Medicine Initiative because of her son with Duchenne Muscular Dystrophy. The President must have mentioned Jillian's name 20 times as an example of how his Community College initiative can help families. The other letter writer was a 14 year old girl who was there with her dad. She wrote about her 11 year old brother with Cystic Fibrosis. What an amazing day. I'll post the photo when we get it from the White House. Joy

HOW WONDERFUL TO BE ABLE TO THANK PRESIDENT OBAMA FOR SAVING ELISE'S LIFE WITH THE ACA- OBAMACARE!

Comment by Joy: January 13, 2018:   We believed Elise would not have had insurance after age 18 if she was not a full time student. That was the experience friends had had, and I had seen this in disability cases we investigate at EEOC under the Americans with Disabilities Act. The effective date of the ACA for the section about covering children until age 26 occurred earlier the same year Elise's mass was found. Therefore we never had the occasion to look at our policy to see when we would have lost coverage for Elise had the ACA not been passed. After I posted this picture, another Federal employee told me our policy already covered children up to age 26. This did not take away the fact that we got to meet President Obama because of my letter thanking him for the ACA. I thank my parents for teaching me to always send thank you notes for gifts.

Marty Pentz, January 21, 2015 · I know that Elise has already posted the wonderful news that her MRI showed no cancer and that the tumor is shrinking. Her and our Miracle continues. Life is such an amazing journey and it is good to be in a joyful run at this time. I have started writing again and using Dragon to save my wrists and arms. Will post how this is going from time to time.

Another great MRI and request for prayers for Marty by Joy Pentz, April 22, 2015: Elise had another stable MRI with a little shrinkage of the benign neoplasm, as the reports now refer to her dead tumor. I never thought I would be happy to see those words in reference to one of my kids, but it is much better sounding than Anaplastic Astrocytoma Grade III. We were quite worried about this MRI because we have noticed Elise dragging her left foot a little and curling her left hand, which had been earlier symptoms. She will be going back to physical therapy for an evaluation and maybe a splint to keep her hand uncurled at night.

Marty recently had pancreatitis, and then a EUS (sonogram) procedure and MRI to rule out cancer. They did not find any "definite focal masses," but could not rule out cancer. The EUS procedure will be repeated May 29, and hopefully they can rule out cancer at that time. He is screened for pancreatic and colon cancer on a regular basis because of his family history, so if it is cancer it will have been detected early. He has started eating a very low fat diet, and is feeling much better. All this waiting and worrying is so stressful. We would really appreciate your prayers. Thanks, Joy

April 23, 2015, by Marty Pentz. As some of you may know Elise's last MRI showed a still decreasing in size benign tumor and no hint of cancer, Yippee!!! In another note I have been having some health issues. A few weeks ago I was experiencing stomach pain and nausea. At the ER I was diagnosed with acute pancreatitis, at least the third time I have known I had this. My GI Dr. ordered an endoscopic ultrasound (EUS) and colonoscopy. Colonoscopy was fine. The EUS was inconclusive due to the inability to see my whole pancreas, MRI did not show it either. Here is the Drs. Statement 1. "Nonvisualization of the distal portion of the main pancreatic duct and the common bile duct. There is increased enhancement in the pancreatic head without definite visualized focal mass, however underlying pancreatic head mass cannot be excluded. Recommend further evaluation with ERCP/EUS...2. Long segment stricture of the pancreatic duct with poststenotic dilation and dilated pancreatic duct sidebranches, compatible with chronic pancreatic. 3. Duodenal Stricture."

I had an ERCP 15 years ago and had a bout of pancreatitis at that time caused by the procedure. There may be more medical terms than needed, but I did not know how else to say this. Plan is to see my GI doctor on the 12th of May to determine how to address chronic pancreatitis, and to see about the necessity of having the follow up EUS with dilation of my small intestine so they can see the head of my pancreas. The risk of the procedure is perforating my small intestine with the complications that ensues. The risk of not doing it is not knowing for sure if I have pancreatic cancer or not. With a family history of pancreatic cancer, so far all recommendations are for me to go forward with the dilation EUS. So far all things point to me not having cancer. My tumor marker for pancreatic cancer is in the normal range. All this technical stuff to keep from sharing the fear Joy and I have been in the past few weeks. After talking with friends, a GI nurse I know at work, Joy doing much research, and prayer we are in a better place emotionally today. I had a small bout with pancreatitis yesterday, but no pain or nausea today. Feel good right now. I have not been sleeping well. Fear is not the absence of faith, faith is what allows me to do what is needed, despite the fear. "Don't move the way fear makes you move. Move the way love makes you move. Move the way joy makes you move." Osho Indian Spiritual Teacher

Great news about Marty by Joy Pentz, May 13, 2015: Thanks for all your thoughts and prayers for Marty and of course Elise. Marty had a CT scan with and without contrast yesterday, and they were able to see everything this time, and there was no tumor. He will have another CT scan in 3-4 months. There was thick scar tissue in his duodenum (small intestine) and scar tissue in the pancreatic duct that is not too bad. The scar tissue in the duodenum is not important unless it is causing pancreatitis due to blockage. They could do another EUS (Endoscopic Ultra Sound) to try to stretch out his duodenum, but there is a risk of perforation. Another option is to do an ERCP procedure to open the valve between his duodenum and pancreas, but there is a risk of causing pancreatitis. Marty had two ERCP procedures 15 years ago and had pancreatitis afterwards both times. The doctor said the scar tissue can both cause pancreatitis and be the result of pancreatitis. We are going to follow the advice of the doctors who met about this, which is to have another CT scan in 3-4 months, but let them know if he has more pancreatitis so the other two options can be reconsidered. I am so grateful and relieved!

Marty Pentz, May 13, 2015: It feels weird to be grateful to have chronic pancreatitis as the alternative is pancreatic cancer. Life is good.

Stable MRI for Elise by Joy Pentz, August 18, 2015: Yippee! Elise had another stable MRI. Thank God. We are now waiting at the brain surgeon's office so she can get her shunt reprogrammed.   Marty had another CT scan due to an ER visit for pancreatitis, and everything looks good. His doctor said he doesn't need to do any scans for a year unless he has a problem.

Another great MRI! By Joy Pentz, November 17, 2015: Thank God for another stable MRI. The blood profusion is still normal, which means the remaining tumor is getting no nutrients to grow. The tumor is a bit smaller. Dr Y, the brain surgeon said, "Slowly but surely it's getting smaller and smaller." I tend to hang on every word, and the word surely makes me think he expects it to continue to shrink. The docs here think we can go six months between MRIs, but Dr. B, Elise's surgeon at the Cleveland Clinic suggests we don't go any longer than four months, so the next one will be March. Today her left foot hopping was almost as strong as her right foot hopping during her exam. It's hard to believe, considering there was a time she couldn't walk or even sit up without falling over. Elise is driving again after being cleared by an occupational therapist who tested her reaction time and distractibility and then drove with her. She has started volunteering at a food pantry for a few hours once a week starting last week. She had to leave a bit early her first day due to fatigue. She takes people around to the different shelves to get the food according to the size of their family.   I am going to England Saturday to help Emily with her baby due November 24. I'll be there for 3 weeks. I hate leaving Elise, but she'll be in good hands with Marty. We are very excited to welcome our new granddaughter and niece into the world.   Thanks to all of you for your support and prayers.

Marty Pentz, November 25, 2015 · 2028 hours: I have not written an update in some time and there is great news to celebrate. I have been bubbling with joy. Elise had an MRI on 17th of November and there is no cancer and the tumor keeps shrinking. She is driving and volunteering one morning per week at a local food pantry. Emily gave birth to our second granddaughter, Ruth Isla (pronounced Eye-la) on the 18th. Mother and daughter are doing wonderfully. Joy flew to England to be with them for the next three weeks. Elise and I miss her, but I am grateful she can be there with Emily, Matthew, Lilia and Ruth.

ELISE'S NIECES, LILIA AND RUTH, SISTER EMILY AND HER HUSBAND, MATTHEW

RUTH AND LILIA - SUMMER 2017 IN WEYHILL, ENGLAND

Elise and I went to see Mary Poppins put on by Center Grove HS and the performance was electrifying. I shed a lot of tears of joy that I could share this with Elise when just a little over three years ago she was close to death and could not walk, talk or breathe on her own. God and Life has been good to me. None of this would have been possible without the recovery programs I have been in since I was 24. Despite the pain love can bring into one's life it is still the only game worth playing. Many years ago I would pray for justice and good, now I know I needed and received mercy from a loving God. "As far as inner transformation is concerned, there is nothing you can do about it. You cannot transform yourself, and you certainly cannot transform your partner or anybody else. All you can do is create a space for transformation to happen, for grace and love to enter." Eckhart Tolle

MRI yesterday by Joy Pentz, March 23, 2016:   Good news and not so good news. Elise had her MRI yesterday, and the tumor remained the same, but the cyst on her tumor got bigger. It is nothing like the size two years ago, so that's good. Elise's oncologist is going to speak with the surgeon at Cleveland Clinic who did the laser ablation surgery to see if cysts going up and down is something he has seen with his other patients. Elise was only patient #19, so there may not be a lot of comparators who have survived long enough to see late effects of the treatment. She also has a pineal cyst that I did not know about, which also got bigger. The doctor said pineal cysts are so common, it wasn't even worth mentioning. They did not do profusion on this MRI because the person who set it up is new and I didn't double check about it like I have always done. That would have been a comfort to know the tumor is still dead without a viable blood supply to feed it. I feel very unsettled and worried.

Neither of the doctors we saw yesterday seemed too concerned, and she is as good clinically as she has always been. The grip on her left hand is stronger than 4 months ago, and she was able to hop on her left foot more times than ever. She is doing lots of puzzles and Lumosity exercises, getting faster at all of them. I recently started reading to her and asking her questions about the details. I am impressed with her short term memory. All of these things are miraculous, and I will try to focus on that. And pray.

Marty has been experiencing nausea just about every time he eats. He will be having ultrasound endoscopy Monday to examine his duodenal stricture and his pancreas. He may have balloon dilation to try to open up the stricture more. In the meantime he is taking pancreatic enzymes and avoiding solid food in favor of smoothies, soggy cereal and eggs to see if that helps. I read about a procedure at Johns Hopkins for chronic pancreatitis used when people are in constant pain. They remove the entire pancreas, harvest the islet of Langerhans cells, which produce insulin, and transplant them into the liver. The liver then produces insulin, and the person does not develop diabetes. Enzymes are taken to substitute for the other function of the pancreas, to help digest food. Thanks to Marty's very restrictive fat free diet, his pain is less often. Pancreatic pain is caused by the pancreatic enzymes not being able to reach the intestines, and instead start digesting the pancreas and causing scarring and fibrosis, which further traps the enzymes. It's good to know there is a possible solution that may be available to him if necessary. Chronic pancreatitis is a very serious disease itself, and increases the chances of developing pancreatic cancer, which his brother died from. I need to focus on the fact that Marty has been followed very closely due to his family history. And pray. While I'm telling you about all our health problems, I just found out I have leukopenia, low white blood cell count. That helps explain why I have been so exhausted. Our dog, Lucy, is in perfect health! Yay! Thanks for your thoughts and prayers. Joy

Marty Pentz, March 23, 2016. · Elise's MRI was good again yesterday, no tumor growth nor cancer. God is good.

Great news for Marty, by Joy Pentz, March 29, 2016:   Great news re Marty. The doctor was able to dilate the duodenal stricture to 15 mm. He should not have food getting stuck and making him nauseous. He said his pancreas looks good other than a bit fatty (they don't know what causes that) and the pancreatic duct is 4 mm and should be 2-4 mm. The condition of his pancreas doesn't qualify for a diagnosis of chronic pancreatitis! They can try to dilate the stricture more (normal is 24 mm) if he still has problems. The opening of the stricture looked pea size before dilation and quarter coin size after the dilation in the lovely pictures they took. Next step is another EUS (endoscopic ultrasound) in a year, which they have already been doing because of his brother having died of pancreatic cancer. They took several biopsies to check for celiac, h pylori, and of course they will note if any cells look like cancer. Marty is so excited to be able to eat solids again. Thank God for health. Thanks for all of your support.

July 29, 2016 by Joy Pentz: Results from MRI July 26. Great news and not so great news. The cyst on Elise's tumor grew, but it is still smaller than it was in April 2014. The great news is that the dead tumor is stable with no change in profusion. Elise's neurooncologist showed us the MRI on her computer screen. I said the tumor looks smaller, and she agreed. She showed us the MRIs from March 2016 and April 2014 when the enlarged cyst first appeared. The shrinking of the tumor from two years ago to now is remarkable. The cyst can grow quite a bit more before reaching its former size, which caused no symptoms. The cyst extends into one of her ventricles, space which holds cerebral spinal fluid. This would normally be worrisome because it could block the flow of fluid, causing pressure in her brain. However, her shunt drains the fluid into her abdomen. Also, the third ventriculostomy procedure, which was her first of four brain surgeries, created a path for drainage that was blocked by the tumor.

Elise's neurooncologist, Dr. Jessica, is the most wonderful doctor, and Elise loves her dearly. We all do. She never lets us go home without first finding out the results of the MRI. She doesn't just read the radiologist reports. She studies her scans carefully, and shows them to us in all different views and slices. When we see her she makes us feel like Elise is her only patient, and she has all the time in the world to visit with us. She remembers details about Elise's life, her boyfriend and family members, and always asks specifics about how everyone is doing. She is a pediatric neurooncologist, and she became Elise's doctor because Elise was diagnosed at age 19. Elise asked her back then how long she could stay with her, and she told her until age 25. That seemed very far away at that time, and her prognosis made it seem unlikely, but Elise will be 25 on her next birthday Feb 29. There has been no talk of passing her on to an adult Doctor, but if there is, we will try pulling the leap year card. Elise has only had six birthdays so far. If she has to leave at age 25, that's ok because it will be about 75 years from now, and Dr. Jessica will probably be retired by then anyway :)

Elise has continued to volunteer at Green Tree retirement center. She is enjoying working with the activities director to create a fairy garden. Thanks to the "other" Suzanne who left a comment about relearning how to balance on a bike, Elise is hopeful she will be able to ride again soon. We bought her a 20 inch bike and removed the pedals. She a practicing coasting and just putting her feet on the ground to stop. Although she was willing to use training wheels, she won't have to, which is good because it's hard to find a set that fits an adult bike.

We are enjoying a visit from Emily and her family. She and Matthew are great parents to Lilia and Ruth, ages 4 and 8 months. Being a grandma is absolutely wonderful, but I can see why children are granted to the young. Elise decided after a few days that she doesn't want any. Daniel and Sara will join us later. I envy those of you who have your children and grandchildren close by.   Thanks again for your support and prayers. Joy

Results from MRI Nov 11, 2016 Journal entry by Joy Pentz — 11/13/2016: Great news! The MRI showed the cyst is now quite a bit smaller than the last MRI, and the dead tumor is stable with no abnormal profusion. In less than a month, Dec 10, Elise will have survived 5 years since her tumor was found. She continues to diligently rehab her brain daily by working puzzles, using Lumosity and exercising 3-4 days per week. Yesterday I read a few magazine articles to her, and asked her questions about them. I was very impressed with her recall ability. The things she did not remember right away, she remembered with hints.

Elise's sleepiness and low stamina issues have not improved significantly. Of course we are hoping these issues are caused by chemo and radiation that sometimes take years to improve. We have to accept that at least part of it may be caused by the brain injury of the tumor and may never normalize. We have set up a special needs trust as part of our wills for this reason. The good news is it is no longer an impossible dream to think she might outlive us.

We have an appointment with her neurologist to see if she can come off her anti-seizure meds. We will ask him about Provigil, which is a drug for narcolepsy that Elise took while she was inpatient at Hook rehab. It helped her stay awake enough to do the therapies that allowed her to walk again and improve her cognitive functioning. Insurance would not pay for it as an outpatient, and it is very expensive. We will try again. As always, thanks for your support and prayers.

Five year milestone!!! Journal entry by Joy Pentz — Dec 10, 2016. It is hard to believe it has been five years since the Physician's Assistant in the emergency room at Riverview Hospital squatted down by our chairs to our eye level to tell us there is a mass in Elise's brain. I asked how big it was and was it operable, and he said, "Whoa. Let's not get ahead of ourselves until we have more information." He asked if we wanted to see the scan, and he took us to a computer to view it. My eyes about popped out and I said, "It's huge!" It was the size of a golf ball deep in her brain.

Elise's boyfriend, Drew, got down on his knees by Elise's bed and cried. The Physician's Assistant told us he ordered the scan because Elise took just a few seconds too long for a 19 year old to answer his questions. Otherwise, her symptoms were headache and vomiting. He could have easily chalked it up to the flu, treated the symptoms and sent us on our way. We went to that small hospital in a different town because we had a sleep study scheduled there because a friend had recommended a doctor there, and we hoped maybe they would do it on an emergency basis. Elise had not been able to stay awake during the day for a while.

As far as we could tell, Elise was the only patient in the ER. If we had gone to the large Indianapolis hospital 10 minutes from home with its busy waiting room, who knows what might have happened? Brain tumors are so rare, and up until then Elise's only symptom had been sleepiness. They transferred us by ambulance to St Vincent Hospital, where our journey continued. I remember riding in the ambulance assuming she was going to die.

The doctor on call told us it looked like a low grade glioma. They don't use the term benign for brain tumors. He told us it would cause too much brain damage to operate. He asked about family history, and we told him about the cancer in Marty's family. When he asked if we had any questions I said, "I can tell by the look on your face, that I won't like the answers." I didn't want to ask any more questions.

Meanwhile, Elise was in the Neuro ICU getting steroids to reduce the pressure in her brain, and she was becoming aggressive and agitated. She was too dehydrated for them to start an IV in her hand, so they had to use her neck. She didn't know what was going on, and we heard her screaming down the hall during the procedure. The nurses came into her room frequently to check on her to make sure she did not go into a coma from the pressure in her brain.

This was on a Saturday, and we had to wait until Monday for surgery. The surgeon told us the tumor caused her third ventricle to be blocked, and the cerebral spinal fluid could not circulate properly, so he was going to perform a third ventriculostomy to reroute it. He was also going to biopsy the tumor. He too thought the tumor was low grade, and said it was too risky to remove a tumor from the thalamus. It took from December 10, 2011 to

January 25, 2012, to find out the tumor was malignant.

Fast forward five years. Today we went to the most wonderful wedding, and Elise was the usher. Later at the reception, she was having so much fun dancing. She worked very hard just to learn how to walk again, and is still working hard to rewire her brain by diligently solving all kinds of puzzles and doing brain training on Lumosity. We marveled at the miracle of the life of our little girl as we watched her dance. It was a great way to spend such an important milestone.

We thank all of you for your support and prayers for the last five years!

Journal entry by Joy Pentz — 4/19/2017. Elise had another MRI today. It showed the tumor to be stable, maybe a bit smaller. The cyst was smaller. Yippee!

Elise started taking Provigil about a month ago to help with her sleepiness. It is a drug used for narcolepsy. She had to have a sleep study to see if she met the criteria for insurance to pay for it. It's quite expensive.

The sleep study didn't show she had narcolepsy, but she was close. She fell asleep 4 of the 5 times they monitored her. It took her an average of 10 minutes to fall asleep. The cutoff is 8 minutes. She didn't have REM sleep during the naps, which is another sign of narcolepsy. I guess the insurance company took pity on her.

Since she started the Provigil, she needs fewer naps, and is more alert and energetic. She says she feels alive again! She thought her tumor would be half the size today because she feels so good.

Thanks for all your prayers and support. Joy

Journal entry by Joy Pentz — 10/25/2017. Elise had an MRI today which showed her tumor to be stable. What a relief. She was supposed to have her MRI October 10, but the profusion MRI machine was not working. About a week before October 10, Elise called me to tell me she vomited and had a bad headache, and she was worried. That's the first time Elise said she was worried about her tumor. She was having the same symptoms she had the day they found the mass. I heard from two friends that there was a virus going around, which really comforted us. We were so relieved when she felt fine in a few days. I had called her doctor, and she said that it was either her tumor, her shunt or a virus. Even though Elise started improving the next day, we were still more apprehensive than we usually are right before her MRI. Having to postpone it two weeks for the MRI repair after having gone the longest planned interval between MRIs, took a toll on our serenity.

I am still nervous because Elise did not remember how to walk from the hospital to the surgeon's office to make sure her shunt was at the correct setting after the MRI. After that, we saw her neuro oncologist, and she showed us the scan compared to the previous one on her computer. She said it looked stable to her, but we had to wait for the radiologist report. Her husband is a radiologist, so she is always able to find one to view the scan and write the report the same day. He also said it looked stable. I will feel better after her surgeon at Cleveland Clinic weighs in because it was hard to tell. The slice of the brain seen on the scan doesn't always match the previous scan, and the tumor is irregularly shaped, and it looked like it could be slightly bigger. Also the radiologist said he couldn't tell much from the profusion shots because of all the dried up blood around the tumor. The radiologist here don't usually use profusion MRI exams so they are not well practiced in interpreting them. The surgeon at Cleveland Clinic is the one who asks for it. My understanding is that it shows whether the tumor has a blood supply, which it needs to become active again, so I always want to get those results. I started this post last night, but

Fell asleep before I finished it. The fact that I am finishing it at 3:00 AM I guess means I am not totally convinced the tumor is still dead because I can't sleep. Thank you all for your thoughts, prayers and support. Good night.

Journal entry by Joy Pentz — 10/26/2017. The doctor called to tell me Elise's labs were good. I told her I didn't feel certain the MRI showed the tumor was stable. She was adamant that she had no doubt and she would tell me if she did. She was very surprised I was doubtful. Anyway, she convinced me everything is ok. I feel much better.

Journal entry by Joy Pentz — 1/7/2018. Happy New Year to everyone. This year December 10 was almost over before we realized it was an anniversary date. We passed 6 years since we found out Elise had a mass in her brain. I guess forgetting it is a sign we are not as fearful about Elise's survival as we once were. That's a good thing. On the 25th of this month, it will be 6 years since we found out the tumor was malignant. We are so grateful, and are looking forward to Elise's work with Voc Rehab and Rehabilitation Hospital of Indiana to figure out a vocation and the training she will need to get it. I was a bit disappointed when I saw her latest assessment, but on second thought, we are so blessed she is alive, and has the abilities she has retained. Thank God her tumor was on the right side of her thalamus so her verbal skills are intact for the most part. She did poorly on retaining lists of words, but she can remember things that have some context like a story. Someone pointed out to me that being able to recite a list of words is not something most people do in everyday life. Thank you all for your thoughts and prayers and all of your support.

On February 11, 2018, Elise celebrated 7 years of being clean and sober! We are all so grateful for the recovery and fellowship that is central to her life. In all likelihood, she would have slipped into a coma and died from her brain tumor, if she had not gotten clean, because she would not have recognized that her symptoms were the result of something besides using and being hung over.

The day before, February 10, 2018, was the 30th anniversary of the day Marty and I met. Obviously, this story of Elise and her recovery from addiction and brain cancer would not exist without our paths having crossed.

I cannot describe my feelings of gratitude!

Afterword by Marty, February 13, 2018:

I met Joy after taking the recommendation of a therapist to try something new like International Folk Dancing. I was learning a dance, when I turned around to see a vision of loveliness walk in holding the hand of her three year old daughter Emily, with 5 year old Daniel lagging behind.

I have always been fascinated by what seems to be the fortuitous nature of life. I believe today that by being awake I can see so much of God's love and grace in the world, and say yes to life. I have reworded a saying I find quite arrogant. Instead of "there but for the grace of God go I," my rewording is, "There but for being awake to the grace of God go I." I believe God's grace is available to all of us. It is my task to accept and use it in a loving and healthy fashion.

Keep hope alive in your life. "Hope is being able to see that there is light despite all of the darkness." Desmond Tutu, and "We must accept finite disappointment, but never lose infinite hope." Martin Luther King, Jr.

ELISE AT 25. SHE PROUDLY WEARS HER TRACH SCAR AS A BATTLE SCAR

Appendix:

Elise's Daily Supplements and Foods Used as Medicine

Disclaimer: The following is a list of supplements and remedies we give Elise to attempt to prevent a recurrence of her cancer. We did not use these items to replace the standard treatments she received. We are not qualified to give any medical advice, and this list is not an attempt to do so. We are simply sharing what we are doing and providing links so that you can explore further if you so desire. Be advised that any substance can have negative side effects, and that the combination of these items with each other and with medications is largely unknown. Read more than one source about each of these items before deciding to try them.

Scientists believe all of us get cancer cells on a regular basis, but we don't all get cancer because the immune system prevents uncontrolled growth of these cells. If you build the immune system back up, and improve the body's internal environment, it should help take care of any cancer cells that form. It can be hopeful to think about cancer cells being seeds that have the potential to grow in a favorable environment, but may not grow if the environment is unfavorable. If the soil is lacking nutrients and/ or the seeds do not get the right amount of moisture or light, the seeds may not germinate or grow. Our hope is that by correcting the environment in Elise's system, there will not be fertile ground for cancer cells to grow into tumors.[2]

---

[2] Info re herbs and spices in cancer prevention and treatment:
https://www.ncbi.nlm.nih.gov/books/NBK92774/

Of course, we don't know which, if any, of these things is keeping Elise's cancer at bay, but our philosophy is if it doesn't hurt and it might help, why not? Although there are unknown risks and benefits with Elise's regimen, we feel the potential benefits outweigh the risk of dying from incurable cancer with dismal statistics when only standard treatments are used.

Joy does the research and keeps the supplements stocked. Marty places them in weekly pill organizers, one for days and another for nights. Elise takes them faithfully, and makes it more enjoyable by creating mosaic pictures with the tablets and capsules before she takes them.

- Ashwaganda[3]
- Astaxanthin[4]
- Baby Aspirin 1X/day[5]
- Bacopa[6]
- Barley leaf extract [7]
- Beta glucan[8]
- Borage Oil[9]

---

[3] https://www.mskcc.org/cancer-care/integrative-medicine/herbs/ashwagandha

[4] Info re Astaxanthin: https://www.ncbi.nlm.nih.gov/pmc/articles/PMC4515619/

[5] https://www.mdanderson.org/publications/focused-on-health/november-2014/low-dose-aspirin-cancer-prevention.html

[6] http://blog.lifeextension.com/2017/06/adaptogen-highlight-bacopa-for-brain.html

[7] http://allonhealth.com/barleylife/barley-juice-references.htm

[8] http://glucan.us/Glucan-relevant-2017.pdf

[9] Info re Borage Oil: http://news.bbc.co.uk/2/hi/health/743774.stm

- **Boswellia**[10]
- **Broccoli Sprout Extract tablets**[11]
- **Calcium with magnesium**[12]
- **Cayenne pepper**[13]
- **Cinnamon**[14]
- **Coenzyme Q 10**[15]
- **Essiac tea – Nurse Rene Caisse from Canada used Objibwe Indian herbal mixture to cure cancer in the 1920's**[16]
- **Flax seed oil in cottage cheese (see below and in foot note)**
- **Flax seeds, whole – chew 1 tsp**[17]
- **Ginger**[18]
- **Goji**[19]
- **Goldenseal root (berberine)**[20]
- **Graviola capsule – from soursop, a fruit related to paw paw – traditional remedy from Asia and South America**[21]
- **Green tea extract**[22]

---

[10] Info re Boswellia: https://www.ncbi.nlm.nih.gov/pubmed/27346540

[11] https://www.mskcc.org/cancer-care/integrative-medicine/herbs/broccoli-sprouts

[12] http://drsircus.com/cancer/magnesium-and-cancer/

[13] https://www.drweil.com/diet-nutrition/cooking-cookware/cooking-with-spices-cayenne-pepper/

[14] https://www.healthline.com/nutrition/10-proven-benefits-of-cinnamon#section8

[15] https://www.cancer.gov/about-cancer/treatment/cam/patient/coenzyme-q10-pdq

[16] To view an old video about the history of Essiac with an interview of Nurse Caisse and her patients go to: http://essiacfacts.com/rene-caisse/

[17] https://www.umm.edu/health/medical/altmed/herb/flaxseed

[18] https://prevention.cancer.gov/news-and-events/news/ginger-helps-reduce-nausea

[19] https://gojijuices.net/goji-juice-research/

[20] https://www.mskcc.org/cancer-care/integrative-medicine/herbs/goldenseal

[21] http://graviolacancers.com/graviola-cancer-research/

- **Krill oil or fish oil**
- **Low dose Naltrexone[23]**
- **Melatonin**
- **Milk thistle extract (sylimarin)[24]**
- **Multiple vitamin/mineral**
- **Mushroom trio capsules (maitake, reishi and shiitake)- used in Asia by cancer doctors[25]**
- **Probiotic[26]**
- **Quercetin with bromelain[27]**
- **Raspberry ketones with white kidney beans tablets[28]**
- **Resverotral with red wine extract**
- **Ruta and cal phos homeopathic meds Dr. Banerji in India uses in his research clinic to treat brain cancer.[29] His clinic daily treats thousands of patients of all illnesses, hundreds for free. I consult free by email, and his clinic has made some modifications to Elise's meds over the years. He has a huge database of results, scans, biopsies etc., and his work has**

---

[22] https://www.umm.edu/health/medical/altmed/herb/green-tea

[23] Info re low dose Naltrexone: https://www.ncbi.nlm.nih.gov/books/NBK390569/

[24] https://www.cancer.gov/about-cancer/treatment/cam/patient/milk-thistle-pdq

[25] Info re mushrooms used for cancer: https://www.ncbi.nlm.nih.gov/pmc/articles/PMC3339609/

[26] https://www.mdanderson.org/publications/focused-on-health/may-2015/FOH-probiotics.html

[27] Info re Quercetin: http://www.mdpi.com/2072-6694/2/2/1288/htm Info re bromelain: https://www.mskcc.org/cancer-care/integrative-medicine/herbs/bromelain

[28] For info re Raspberry: https://www.ncbi.nlm.nih.gov/pubmed/26773014; for info re beans: http://naturalsociety.com/eating-certain-beans-cuts-risk-5-cancers/

[29] For Banerji brain tumor case studies with MRI scans go to: http://www.pbhrfindia.org/case-studies-at-pbhrf/brain-tumor-or-cancer-casestudies.html

been peer reviewed by MD Anderson and National Cancer Institute.[30]
- **Sea Kelp**[31]
- **Selenium**[32]
- **Spirulina**[33]
- **Turmeric/curcumin**[34]
- **Vitamin D3**[35]
- **Vitamin E**[36]

Additional Items no longer given daily:

- **Aloe arborescens detox (earlier) Father Zago learned from Brazilian Natives as a cure**[37]

---

[30] Paper entitled 'Cancer patients treated with The Banerji Protocols utilizing homoeopathic medicine: A Best Case Series Program of the National Cancer Institute USA'., Prasanta Banerji, Donald R. Campbell and Pratip Banerji; Oncology Reports 20: 69-74, 2008. Read the paper at: http://www.pbhrfindia.org/images/publications/pbhrf_final_published_paper___o ncology_reports_2008.pdf

[31] http://www.seaweed.ie/medicine/seaweedcancer.php

[32] https://www.pcrm.org/health/cancer-resources/diet-cancer/nutrition/how-selenium-helps-protect-against-cancer#main-content

[33] https://www.umm.edu/health/medical/altmed/supplement/spirulina

[34] https://www.umm.edu/health/medical/altmed/herb/turmeric

[35] https://www.cancer.gov/about-cancer/causes-prevention/risk/diet/vitamin-d-fact-sheet

[36] https://ods.od.nih.gov/factsheets/VitaminE-Consumer/

[37] Several books have been written on the Aloe Arborescens protocol. A Catholic priest, Father Romano Zago, OFM, developed the official protocol and wrote the

- **Baking soda and molasses in cup of water (for lessening alkalinity) 1 tsp each 2X/day (earlier)[38]**
- **Liposomal vitamin C (earlier) (coated with lecithin to survive digestion)[39]**
- **Salvestrol (earlier)[40]**

Juice/Food used as medicine daily

V8 Splash Peach/Mango (8oz= 1 serving of fruit and 1 serving of vegetables- no sugar or high fructose corn syrup) Elise drinks twice a day to swallow meds.[41]

book on the history of the cure and details of its use. This book is called: Cancer Can Be Cured! The book has a long list of impressive case studies for different kinds of cancer. https://www.amazon.com/gp/offer-listing/B01FKWH43S/ref=sr_1_9_olp?ie=UTF8&qid=1517877329&sr=8-9&keywords=cancer+can+be+cured

[38] http://cancerstopped.blogspot.com/2012/05/baking-soda-and-cancer-cells.html

[39]How to make Liposomal Vitamin C at home. https://www.bing.com/videos/search?q=how+to+make+liposomal+vit+c+at+home&qpvt=how+to+make+liposomal+vit+c+at+home&FORM=VDRE

[40] Info re Salvestrol: http://orthomolecular.org/library/jom/2007/pdf/2007-v22n04-p177.pdf

[41] See the Angiogenesis Foundation website at: https://angio.org/

There are certain foods, including peaches, apples and certain types of teas, which are known to have anti-angiogenic properties. Anti-angiogenic means they help prevent the growth of new blood vessels. Once tumors reach a certain size they cannot sustain themselves without forming new blood vessels to keep them alive. The only time the formation of new blood vessels is desirable is during pregnancy. One of the drugs Elise took, Avastin (bevacizumab), does the same thing. She had infusions of Avastin every other week for a year.

Raw vegetables – carrots, bell pepper, cucumber, squash, cruciferous veggies like broccoli, spinach

Fresh, frozen or dried fruit[42]

Nuts – Walnuts, pecans or almonds[43]

Coconut oil/oatmeal mini muffin[44]

Cottage cheese with flaxseed oil – Dr. Budwig protocol[45]

---

[42] Info re vegetables, fruits and other complementary treatments/preventions: https://www.theguardian.com/education/2002/sep/10/science.highereducation

[43] https://www.drfuhrman.com/learn/library/articles/109/nuts-and-seeds-help-keep-disease-away

[44] http://www.doctoroz.com/article/surprising-health-benefits-coconut-oil

[45] Germany's Dr. Johanna Budwig's cottage cheese and flaxseed oil protocol. We add fruit or jelly without sweetener and cinnamon for taste. This must be eaten immediately after mixing. We mix about 4 T of cottage cheese with 1 T flaxseed oil for every 100 pounds of body weight. We did not do this until April 2014 when the cystic portion of Elise's dead tumor grew very quickly between MRIs. She was scheduled for surgery two weeks later and the surgery was cancelled when the pre-operative MRI showed it was ¼ the size. An MRI 6 weeks later showed no cyst at all. Dr. Budwig was an expert in lipids who discovered that most of the processed oils we use tend to clog cell membranes causing disease, but flaxseed oil actually cleared the membranes making them permeable again and able to communicate with other cells and use the enzymes etc. to keep our immune system healthy to kill cancer cells we all get before they become tumors. All of Elise's doctors were amazed at how the cyst disappeared without rupturing and causing problems. I didn't give this to Elise before the cyst because she hates cottage cheese, but I went into panic mode with the cyst and potential regrowth of her dead tumor, and convinced her to try it with the flavor

enhancements. Now she actually likes it. Update: a much smaller cyst grew in the same place in her July 2016 MRI, but was even smaller on her Nov 2016 MRI. October 2017 MRI showed the cyst is still shrinking.

For more information on Dr. Budwig's research, go to: https://books.google.com/books?id=T2rEtO6dWDAC&dq=Flax+Oil+as+a+True+Aid+Against+Arthritis%2C+Heart+Infarction%2C+Cancer+and+Other+Diseases+Author+Johanna+Budwig&focus=searchwithinvolume&q=Flax+Oil+as+a+True+Aid+Against+Arthritis%2C+Heart+Infarction%2C+Cancer+and+Other+Diseases+Author+Johanna+Budwig Dr. Budwig is considered to be the foremost authority on the role of fats in healing. Translated for the first time in English these lectures by Dr. Budwig, have brought about scientific revolution. Dr. Budwig shows the relationship between cancer and fat metabolism.

Made in the USA
Columbia, SC
29 April 2022

59705708R00102